To: Alex

May your journey
be Transforming

Jerry Wellm

3/24/22

Reflections of a Prison Chaplain:

Narratives of Transformation

Reflections of a Prison Chaplain:

Narratives of Transformation

Chaplain Jerry Welborn

Imaginal Publishing
College Grove, TN

ISBN-9781091888562

xi

In Memory of Chaplain Ben Cobb

CONTENTS

CONTENTS

ACKNOWLEDGEMENTS

A transforming ministry is what this book is about. These experiences have carried me through a profoundly rewarding career. Thus, I deem it important to give special thanks to a few whose help was fundamental to this project. Without their help and support this ministry would not have been possible.

Imagine being twelve or thirteen years old and telling your Sunday school teacher, "I'd rather be fishing than here." I am that person. Had it not been for existential philosophy and my lovely wife, Sarah, who I met in an undergraduate logic class, I would never have dreamed of becoming a minister, much less a chaplain. Having the notion that church was somehow existential, she was the one who asked, "Why don't you go to seminary?" For over fifty years, Sarah and I have collaborated in a spiritual tapestry that joins our lives. Often, we think the same thoughts at the same time. She is as much a part of this book as I am. In addition, she accomplished the heroic task of editing this book. These stories and reflections would never have been formed into a book without the help and encouragement of my soul-mate, Sarah. She is the gift of Ariadne, the thread that affirms life in the presence of a great labyrinth.

Bishop Kenneth Carder of the United Methodist Church Tennessee Conference endorsed my appointments at the

Turney Center Industrial Prison and Farm located in Only, Tennessee and the Riverbend Maximum-security Institution in Nashville, Tennessee. He also endorsed my continuing education for the purpose of carrying out prison ministry. Most importantly, Bishop Carder himself had an active ministry to death row. He opposed capital punishment. Bishop Carder visited Riverbend, met our warden, encouraged our residents, and was often vocal about the local churches reaching out to the incarcerated.

Two men from Christ United Methodist Church in Brentwood, Tennessee, heard that call, Harry Boyko and Jerry Nail. These men brought a Disciple Bible Study to our residents and then followed through with a dynamic program involving their church in mentoring residents and helping them make a successful transition from prison. Bishop Carder, Harry Boyko and Jerry Nail were and are "hands on" in their approach to serving the "least of these."

I started my ministry at Riverbend, was transferred to Turney Center, and then returned to Riverbend where I retired in 2011. A successful program is not possible without a warden who promotes and supports religious and volunteer services. Deputy Warden Ricky Bell and I were present when Riverbend went into operation. In short, we were both transferred to Turney Center and then returned to Riverbend. Comparing Turney Center to Riverbend, I recall him saying this about Riverbend, "It runs itself." I would agree that Riverbend tended to be self-organizing, partly due to the way it was set up as a panopticon, a central structure of observation, in the maximum-security units.

More importantly, Ricky Bell did not micro-manage his staff. He allowed department heads to do their jobs. One day I met with Bell on the ball field and casually suggested that our volunteers needed to meet with maximum-security inmates at their cells, carry in collapsible camp chairs, an bring religious services through the pie-flap---an opening---in the cell door. He agreed to give it a try. It worked; our problems were seldom and minor. This is not something that is carried out under the present administration. Volunteers now stand at the resident's door and speak through a secure window. Officers and staff are now required to wear a face shield when direct contact is made with the maximum-security inmate. I know this because I returned to Riverbend as an interim chaplain after my retirement.

Warden Bell met with college administrators and educators. Harmon Wray and Richard Goode brought Vanderbilt Divinity School to our volunteer program. Later, Richard Goode brought educators from David Lipscomb University. Tennessee Prison Ministry Outreach (TPOM) brought faith-based courses to help our residents acquire successful social skills. Volunteer professors from Middle Tennessee State University brought in a literary study entitled The Great Books. Members of the community helped to establish Narcotics Anonymous and Alcoholics Anonymous meetings. The list goes on. Without Warden Bell a robust volunteer services program would have been slow in coming. Given the shortage of staff and the difficulty of moving a high security inmate, Religious Services for the maximum-security population would have been next to impossible. Currently, programming in the Tennessee Department of Correction is much more 'top-down' than 'bottom-up'. Many thanks to Warden Ricky Bell for his contribution in creating a bridge, a meaningful opportunity, for the inmates and volunteers to examine and carry out what they are truly about—empowering others for transformation.

From 1989 through the fall of 1998, the chaplain's office at Riverbend had no clerical help. In other words, the chaplain had no resident/inmate clerk to help with typing and record-keeping, etc. I made the request to our warden and the request was approved. For the remaining 10 or more years of my tenure at Riverbend, David Phipps served as my clerk. David was much more than a keeper of records, although he did that very well. David had a genuine concern for the resident population and the desire to serve God. He helped to build our program at Riverbend. When Harry Boyko and Jerry Nail came out to sell their Disciple Bible Study Program, I wasn't sold on another Bible study. I remember

David and his friend Buster saying, "We need this program." I reluctantly went along with it. To my surprise, these volunteers followed through with helping the class participants when they were released. You could say that they went the extra mile.

David did 25 years on a life sentence before being released on parole. He never had a disciplinary write-up. He earned a college degree and then a graduate degree while in prison.

Upon release, he continued his affiliation with Tennessee Prison Ministry Outreach. Today, he is on staff with this outstanding organization. He is also completing his Doctor of Ministry degree at David Lipscomb University. We have many stories to share. I am blessed that God sent David to Riverbend to help "set in order the things that are wanting" (Tit 1:5).

INTRODUCTION

I served as chaplain for the Tennessee Department of Correction for 21 years, then retired in August of 2011. I came back and served as an interim chaplain, but that's another story. Many of my retired friends have either traveled or written a book, or both. I have done neither. Yet, there is a pressing need to share with you some of my most extraordinary experiences that I would call surprises. A surprise happens to you; it is not something you're looking for; you run into it or it runs into you. A surprise is not something that one can orchestrate. Such experiences can be transforming.

An example of what I'm talking about happened over a span of twenty-five years. When Riverbend opened in 1989, the new employees went through training on location before any inmates arrived. Lieutenant Tommy Vance was part of that training and his idea was to introduce new recruits to a "real convict." He brought in this, so called, "convict" to give a talk in the chow-hall packed with new recruits. I even remember the inmate's name, Hugh Lee.

Lt. Vance saw it coming. Hugh Lee called on me to stand up, then asked, "Chaplain, who do you work for?"

"I'm employed by the State of Tennessee," I replied

"No, Chaplain, you work for God!" The place cracked up. "That's the problem with chaplains. You're all conformed to serving a broke system!"

Over all of the years, Tommy Vance would jokingly remind me of my wake-up call: "Chaplain, who do you work for?"

Tommy and I retired about the same time. His last work assignment was unit manager on death row. While making my rounds, I stepped into his office for a visit and his usual reminder about who I worked for. As the conversation continued, concerning retirement, Tommy told me that he'd draw retirement from the state and go to work for CoreCivic, a prison-for-profit under construction near Hartsville. A year or so later, I heard that Tommy was working in the central office downtown. I called him at his office. When he answered his state cell phone, I turned the question on him, "Who do you work for, Tommy?"

He knew right away I was on the other end. Referring to his short stint at CoreCivic, he replied, "You can't imagine how bad it was, Chaplain. You'd have to be there to see it for yourself. I can't describe it to you."

Tommy Vance lived into a surprise. He walked into his own question, "Who do you work for?" Work is not all about making money or warehousing human flesh or having both a retirement check and a paycheck.

When I came to work in the prison system, I was like a fish out of water. I had to live into the answer, and that's what a surprise often leads to---an answer in the way of a transforming moment. Tommy Vance experienced a surprise. "I can't describe it to you." It could have been a transforming moment. The apostle Paul never expected to be blinded by a light or hear the voice of Christ: "Saul, Saul, why are you persecuting me?" The experience changed his life. My surprise experiences led me to a stronger faith. All of us, I do believe, have many of these moments, but we are so caught up in everyday life and its distractions that we dismiss them as anomalies or coincidences.

Introduction

In his book, *Healing Fiction*, James Hillman tells us that the plots of our lives do not necessarily unfold in the same sequential manner as one might expect in a story.[1] The story is a sequence of events. The king dies and then the queen dies are the events of a story. The plot answers the question "why": the queen died of a broken heart. The answer to the question "why" is the theory. We like answers to stories because they give insight, resolution or closure. Our theories may not be entirely satisfactory or final. Plots of stories often fit neatly in a mold, but the plots of our lives may not. Hollywood can tell a story by way of conventions like twelve stages in Joseph Campbell's hero's journey. Men in prison have stories that do not make it to the third stage of the journey: meeting of the mentor. Many of them, in fact, have not grown up with a father, a mother or grandparents who could have offered substance for their souls.

My reflections on and direction into mystery may make one think that I am a relic or something out of the past, and that may be. I simply want my faith to make sense in a world that appears to worship rationality and materialism. In addition, my efforts are not so much a need to convince the world of a mystery as it is a need to explore and celebrate the personal events and relationships as they have unfolded or enfolded within the nexus of my own narrative.

As I write these words, I hope to encourage those who are incarcerated. Whatever the difficulty, take courage, don't give up. Believe in yourself because you belong to a universe that works for the good of all. Never doubt that you are unique and have a future. Believe in virtue and strive to achieve it within the context of the human community. The most important lesson in life is to acquire the wisdom, the skill and the ability to discern right from wrong and act on it. And this, I believe, is at the heart of an authentic personal narrative. For me, it is also the heart of Christian faith.

---

[1] James Hillman, *Healing Fiction* (Woodstock, CT: Spring Publications, 1983), 9-12.

In the story entitled, "The Calling," who would think that at the beginning of my job as chaplain I would meet someone I had known earlier in my life. Like my friend, Tommy Vance, I am confronted with my own history in a compelling realization that leads to a choice.

"The Pipe Puffing Chaplain" is a story about a man who set me on my path. This book is in memory of that person, Chaplain Ben Cobb.

Early on I met a resident named Harris Hatfield. Right after I retired, Harris was released on parole. I played a part in his parole plan. From 1989 through the present we have carried on an extended conversation. "Rhodes Scholar or Road Scholar?" is a chapter about that conversation.

We've all heard that life can be stranger than fiction. How about a staff member who heralds his own death and preaches his own funeral? "Can People Choose How They Cross Over" is that story?

"A Mock Execution" is my own account of what it's like to go through the steps leading to lethal injection. In "The Execution of Sedley Alley," I asked him how it felt to be in this situation; he said that he could only describe it If he made it back to the unit. This was his last visit to death watch.

The evening before Sedley's execution, food was served in the administration building. Some compared it to a party before the enacting of a ritual event. After the execution, witnesses and staff crossed checkpoint with shocked looks on their faces. Sedley's two children were in tears. I was numb, horrified and couldn't sleep that night.

The following day I found myself in the deputy warden's office. He expressed his shock at witnessing Sedley's two children "crying, carrying on and 'slinging snot' on the glass partition" as they watched the state execute their father. I respect the deputy warden because, under all that prison veneer, he could feel something and expressed those feelings. He had no problem retiring a few years later.

"Unintended Consequences: The Death Penalty's Impact on Correctional Staff" takes up the topic of restorative justice. Restorative justice is about changing the way people think about crime and punishment. Harmon Wray and Richard Goode brought the subject of restorative justice to the residents at Riverbend. They taught that people are redeemable.

"A Skunk, A Shoe and a Book" is a personal reflection on synchronicity that prepares the reader for what's to come. It is an attempt to sketch a description and explanation of what happens when we enter the narrative of another and are transformed and mystified by it. The chapters, "A Surprise Reunion," "Captain to the Bridge," "The Execution of Sedley Alley" and "The Execution of Cecil Johnson" are such stories.

"Learning is Reciprocal!" is a description of how I have been blessed by sharing stories with men in prison who desire to live out the concept of "know thyself." A small group met in my office at Turney Center and began reading the dialogues of Plato. Looking through the lens of Plato's mythos, I reflected on the psyche of these men. The outcome of this group was thrilling. These men made their own contribution. They wrote their hearts out. With the exception of spelling errors and minor grammatical changes, I have left these stories and poems as they were written. As I recall, most of these writings were turned in to me typed. In 1999 Warden Ricky Bell allowed a printing of these essays and stories in an unpublished book entitled, *Learning to Live: Journey of Spirit and Soul*.

My friend and teacher, Dr. John Killinger, wrote a foreword to the *Learning to Live* book reminding us that the "finest insights about living have, in fact, come out of prisons." John affirmed the creativity and self-esteem of those who shared their stories. Even as I write this, John has been corresponding with a person from our group. John writes, "In a few remarks this man makes about his existence in prison, and in the things I read between the lines, it is easy to see how completely dehumanizing prison life can be, especially for a person of considerable background and sensitivity."

I connect with all those whose writings have been included in this work. S.R. Hudson in "Heroic Justification" tells the story of a bully who is beat to death with a baseball bat. The bully is a Pee-Wee league coach. I had my own personal experience with a high school baseball coach I watched bully members on his team. One incident resembled the account in Hudson's story, without the murder, of course. Years later, this coach ended up coaching college basketball in Tennessee and eventually was convicted of gambling, an offense which involved sports. Hudson's story tells me that my instincts were on target. I had avoided this coach and the teams under his charge.

"The Laxative" is an interesting and amusing reflection by Mike Stanfield of an eight-year-old boy whose teacher prevents him from leaving class for the restroom. This story hit home when I remembered an incident in the seventh-grade when I needed to go to the restroom. Approaching the teacher's desk, I asked for the pass. She asked, "Do you really have to go?" I replied, "If I didn't need to go, I wouldn't have asked." The teacher slapped me across the face with stunning force. The crack of her hand against my face lifted the faces of the class. I remember their expressions to this day. Now, I ask, "What was her story? What thoughts and emotions would lead to such an act against a seventh-grade student?" Whatever she was thinking or feeling, her story needed to be amended.

In the telling of his story, Mike Stanfield is revisioning these repressive experiences. Likewise, I had to revision my own story. Some years later, I learned that my seventh-grade teacher died of cancer. She had a loving husband and a young child. For me, the choice of a healing fiction, shifting the point of view, caused a release of anger and resentment. Story, as healing fiction, connects our lives with forgiveness and ushers in the joy of God.

I remember the passionate Phillip Jordon and his personal stories of adventure and romance. He was the 'bird man' of the Turney Center chapel. Phillip rescued a baby sparrow. I watched this sparrow land on his shoulder as he entered the chapel; I watched it fly away when he left. He fashioned a bird cage out of popsicle sticks and we harbored her in the chapel until she found her wings, took to flight, never to return. Phillip's essay, "I Have an Answer," is directed to our youth. His answer to despair and violence hits the mark. Young people require the care and wisdom of mentors. Major Gary Phelps served as a chaplain in the United States Air Force. Based on Gary's religious training, he writes about "Natural law into the Millennium." Simply stated, natural law affirms universal standards and principles. Natural law is a construct; it is not like the force of gravity. Perhaps it points to a Platonic form or a unified field. Maybe it points to intelligent design that is far beyond anything within human comprehension.

Gary affirms a democratic way of life which is created by consensus. Problem is that the 'advantage of the stronger' (group consensus) is not always written with a capital 'T'. In this postmodern era the theory of natural law is a dinosaur. That you have your opinion and I have mine can be equated with sophistic relativism. Gary insists on collective integrity and setting standards that stretch humanity beyond the limits of human law and understanding. In so doing, a good and rational argument is maintained. It may be that, in part, we do 'make it up' as we go along, but making it up, under natural law, is not confined to one's own self-interests.

Gray Wolf changed the focus of the group from natural law to his concept of "The Natural Way." Gray Wolf affirms Native American traditions, especially in his desire to live in peace and harmony with nature and his brothers.

The final reflection, "Summary as Inscape," is about story in general, and my story in particular. It takes into account imagination and the power of imagination to drive our choices. My own narrative takes into account these prison stories. They are transforming moments---convictional experiences. We live into these moments and make important decisions and choices. My personal choice has been to take on the Gospel story and walk in faith.

Jerry Welborn
March 7, 2019

THE CALLING

And their eyes were opened, and they knew him; and he vanished out of their sight. Luke 24:31

Riverbend has four housing units in a quadrangle and these units house maximum-security inmates. Currently, housing unit 4 contains a portion of inmates who are close custody, meaning they have come off the highest security level. Unit 2 houses the death row inmates. This area, consisting of these four housing units, is called the 'high side'. What is referred to as the 'low side' contains two housing units, units five and six. These are not and were not classified as high-security areas. The 230 or so inmates housed in unit six are, for the most part, support staff for the facility. Some may be trustees.

A bonified maximum-security inmate is locked down 23 out of 24 hours a day. They are taken out for exercise one hour a day. Inmates who are difficult to manage in prison find their way to maximum-security units. Residents are generally not brought to maximum-security due to the crimes they have committed.

I didn't know what to expect when I met with new arrivals. The head chaplain suggested making rounds. "Make your rounds on the units. Make yourself available to the men."

I walked into unit 5 and then into pod B one afternoon. Several medium-security inmates, maybe 8 or 9, were out of their cells sitting cross-legged in a semicircle on the concrete floor. They were all glaring at me. They sensed my newness and trepidation, so I thought. In the center of the group sat a young thin shirtless man with long blond hair flowing down his back. His hair made him stand out. There was something about his appearance that caught my attention and I didn't quite know what to make of it. I thought he might be a jail-house guru with a following.

"Who are you?" someone asked.

"Chaplain," I said.

The interesting-looking young man with the long hair looked directly at me and exclaimed, "I know you!" I wondered, "Who in the world is this guy?" For the life of me, I could not recognize him. After a pause, I asked, "How do you know me?"

He calmly replied, "You were my scout master."

That happened in 1975, 14 years earlier. He'd grown up and I didn't have a clue which scout addressed me that day.

"I'm Neal, Benny's son," he said.

"I would have never guessed," I said. "How in the world did you come to prison?"

Neal told me the story of how and why he came to prison. His time was short and he anticipated being released soon. I remembered his father, Benny, who served as the assistant scout master. His father had died about ten years earlier of a sudden heart attack. I asked Neal how his brother, Little Benny, was doing.

"He's dead," Neal said.

"I had no idea," I said. "I'm shocked and so sorry to hear that."

"...murdered outside of Tracy City," he went on. "...run over and over by this guy in his car...wanted to make it to look like an accident....got off scot free, got away with murder."

I remembered the pleasant disposition of Neal's mother, Rosy. I told Neal that we still used the quilt that his mother had made and given to us. "Well, Neal, how is your mother getting along through all this?"

"It's very difficult for her."

I offered to help Neal with a call home. Neal refused the call home.

"Does your mother not have a phone?" I asked.

"It's not that," he said. "Mom's in prison."

Absolutely shocked, I said. "Excuse me, I can't imagine such a thing about your mother."

Neal told me that his mother had gone to prison for shooting the young man who allegedly killed Little Benny. As Neal recounted the story, I remembered that his mother worked in a shirt factory. She had never been in trouble, always family-minded and hardworking.

Neal said that his mother just didn't gun the guy down. It all built up over time. This person would come to the parking lot of the shirt factory and taunt Rosy about her deceased son. Rosy knew he would return to taunt her again, so she brought a hand gun to work. The young man returned to the parking lot after work, came over to Rosy's car, got up in her face and she shot him. He dropped dead in the parking lot of the shirt factory where she had worked for many years.

I visited Neal in unit 5 until he left the prison which was not long after our first meeting. Of course, I tried to encourage him the best I could. Rosy's case was on appeal and, as I recall, it wasn't long before she was released from prison.

This story came as a shock. Rosy was the one who kept the family together, the one who constantly insisted on keeping her husband and the boys out of trouble. She worked and maintained a home.

I tried to bring together in my mind what I had learned. First, the encounter and the overall narrative was totally unexpected. I asked myself, "Where did this come from?" I was looking upon a string of events that I didn't want to believe.

Returning to the chapel, I told the older chaplain what had happened. Puffing on his pipe, he casually remarked, "One thing leads to the next and someone goes to jail.

Consider the encounter your initiation. Welcome to Riverbend."

Did Chaplain Cobb see a lesson that I needed to see? Although it was a moving experience, I didn't see anything like a burning bush in housing unit five.

I continued to ponder what had happened. Benny and Rosy embraced positive values and hope. This loving family brought their boys into an organization of discipline, an organization with laws and slogans like "do a good turn daily, help people at all times, be reverent, trustworthy, loyal, helpful, friendly" and so forth. The father, Benny, was not one to drop his sons off at a scout meeting; he participated in the event. The mother had a steady job in a shirt factory, working to help make ends meet.

Two images flashed repeatedly within my mind. The most frequently occurring image was the unrecognized person whom I took for a prison guru, Neal. In an alternate image I caught a glimpse of a shirtless young man lying dead on the black asphalt pavement of a parking lot.

Upon arriving home that evening, I spoke to, Sarah, my wife. "You'll never guess who I ran into this afternoon." She heard me tell the story beginning to end.

Sarah said, "The One who knows you, the One whom you do not recognize, is the Christ. Welcome home. You've finally come into a ministry that fits, take it on."

As I was writing this piece, I glanced out my office window and saw a bright red cardinal. His color was stunning. I grabbed my smart phone and looked up 'cardinal.' Cardinal comes from the Latin word *cardo*, meaning hinge or axis. Christ is the hinge on which the doors of life swing.

THE PIPE PUFFING CHAPLAIN
He Used Rocket Fuel;
I Breathed Pure Oxygen

In 1989 I took on the position of Associate Chaplain at the Riverbend Maximum-security Institution in Nashville, Tennessee. The head chaplain, the man who would become my mentor for the next two years, assigned me to the job of coordinating volunteer services. Between the two of us, we put together a program of religious services and brought in volunteers to serve in these groups. These groups included Protestants, Catholics, Muslims, Buddhists and Native Americans. In time, other group activities would be added to the mix, some of which would be of a secular nature, as in education.

At the time, I was forty-four years old. My previous experience had been in the United Methodist Church preaching and pastoring in rural areas. I had previously worked in local jails, but not in a prison.

Ben Cobb, this balding, mild-mannered and quiet pipe puffing head chaplain, told me why I had been chosen to work as a chaplain. The Riverbend Maximum-security Institution had just been built. This new prison, a prison that would house Tennessee's death row inmates, would have policies and procedures that would be unlike the procedures practiced at the old Main Prison. The administrative staff wanted a fresh

7

approach to running a prison. I was new to prison work and agreed to lend myself to a fresh approach.

At first, I learned how the administration wanted the prison to be run. The warden, Mike Dutton, had worked in the treatment side of incarceration. Ricky Bell was the associate warden. His primary experience was in security. At Riverbend there would be a balance between treatment and security. On the one hand, security had to be maintained through having boundaries, but the boundaries had to be harmonized with programs that would help the resident, such as programs in adult basic education, wood shop, janitorial training and print shop skills. The overall goal was the same then as it is today: helping residents to acquire skills that would enable them to survive in the free world and not reoffend.

One change for a fresh approach was to improve the image of those staff members who played a direct role in their relations to the resident. There are six housing units at Riverbend. All housing unit managers, the unit counselors and the inmate relations coordinators (IRCs) wore a burgundy sport coat and black-tie outfit. Correctional staff wore the standard uniform. Chaplains wore tie and regular street clothes as did the teachers. This change in dress for members of the unit staff suggested 'professionalism,' something other than that of maintaining security and dishing out punishment. A correctional motto went something like: "We're not here to punish the inmate; incarceration is the punishment."

Coming back to Ben's story, I learned about his background before he became a chaplain. You've heard it said, "That's not rocket science." Well, in this case, I was looking right at a rocket scientist. Ben had been one.

Chaplain Ben Cobb told stories of setting off rockets with Wernher von Braun in the early 50's down in Huntsville, Alabama. One story involved hanging onto the swinging ladder of a moving fire truck on the way to a rocket site. I could imagine young Ben Cobb gripping the hook and ladder for dear life while leaving a trail of smoke with his lit pipe held firmly between his teeth.

Several times I visited Ben at his home. He'd be out back, on his patio, puffing that pipe while gazing at an assortment of miniature windmills that he'd fashioned from odds and ends in his garage. These windmills would pivot as the wind touched their unusual-looking blades, some turning faster and others slower, often moving in different directions. Ben talked about chaotic wind currents moving across the ground level of his backyard and marveled at the mystery of it all. I marveled at a man who could make a simple toy windmill and delight in watching it work.

Ben had an insightful sense of humor. He noticed that many residents never thought about the law before coming to prison. While in prison the law was all they could think about. If the law got them in prison, then the law could get them out. Thus, a new 'religion' takes form in prison. Ben called this new religion 'Litigion'. Law books replace sacred texts. The courthouse replaces churches and temples of worship. The ritual garb of religious services takes on the garb of the courthouse. Like the Sophists, some residents practice law for money and not for justice.

One day, Ben was musing about database design. I turned to him and remarked, "This is a skill inmates can learn."

Ben pointed to an inmate who worked in an office down the hall from us and remarked, "Fred used his computer skills to commit fraud. One thing led to the next and fraud became murder. The windmill of life spins and where it stops nobody knows."

I laughed. "You don't really believe that now, do you, that life is unpredictable?"

"I believe this," he replied. "It's more important to learn 'how to think' than 'what to think'. Learning 'how to think' takes on a moral dimension. Without a moral rudder and sail a person is set adrift, carried by the wind and current into a place like this."

On another day, Ben and I were on the way to death row. I can't remember the reason why. I do remember the

9

staff in that unit having difficulty managing a psychotic resident. I asked Ben, "Do you suppose that any of those guys on death row fake mental illness, thinking it will get them off the hook?"

"You never know." He stopped, puffed on his pipe, then turned and looked me in the eye. "I do know this. You fake something long enough, you're liable to catch it. Any habit is hard to break."

I later asked Ben how he ever got interested in prison ministry. While living in Alabama, he attended a church that had a prison ministry. He started visiting inmates, a habit he never broke.

One of our associates, Chaplain Amos Wilson, said, "Ben has the best analytical mind of anyone I've ever met." Ben's ability to analyze and organize was seen right from the start. Ben wrote a database program that kept our religious and volunteer services in order. This order included keeping track of the resident population as well. In addition, Ben designed and wrote a computer program that tracked all the keys in the prison.

Ben offered his prison database program to other chaplains throughout the state in order to help them track volunteer services and keep inmate records. There were no takers. Later, when the state set out to develop its own information system for volunteer services, the Director of Volunteer Services called several chaplains down to the central office to give this new program a spin, and to get our feedback.

At the time, Ben had recently retired and I had taken his place at Riverbend. I went downtown to give this new system a spin along with my feedback. I certainly hoped the spin would not be like a spinning wheel going nowhere. I advised the director to have the programmer consult Ben in order to improve the design. He never did. Even today, fifteen years later, the volunteer information system is seriously flawed. Had they listened, a weekly, monthly or annual report to the commissioner or governor would always be up-to-date, providing the state chaplains used it.

Ben gave the best that he had but never pushed it on others. Ben had patience and tolerance for inmates. Even better, he practiced the habit of patience and tolerance for those on the highest level. Ben drew invisible lines in the sand. I watched closely how he reacted to others.

It was at a training session in Tullahoma that Ben demonstrated his database to the other chaplains in the state. As I said, there were no takers. Surprised, I asked Ben, "Why would a chaplain not want to use a computer program rather than doing the paperwork by hand?"

I told Chaplain Cobb, "It just doesn't make any sense for a chaplain to crank out all the records by hand."

"Yes, that's right," he replied. "Some of these guys may not be keeping records at all or following policy guidelines. You need to let it go. We can't control the habits of our colleagues."

I did let it go. The seed had been cast and landed on rocky soil. What could I say, "Kick the dust off your feet and move on?"

I had a memorable experience during one of those annual training sessions in Tullahoma. I read a work of fiction to the group, something that I'd written about the creation account in *Genesis*. One chaplain was so offended that he stomped out of the room. Puffing on his pipe, Ben smiled and casually remarked, "Put the story on Mars." Ben referenced C.S. Lewis. This simple comment, "Put the story on Mars," made a lasting impression on me. I would stew on it and mull it over in my imagination: "Put it on Mars, put it on Mars." Ben had made his mark on me again.

At Ben's home he demonstrated a flight simulator. I can see him now, sitting behind his computer flying to some distant place.

Ben liked music, and I recall him tinkering with a program that synthesized it. He played a tune that he had written. It was interesting how Ben could tinker with the keyboard and come up with various sounds. I asked, "Can you make the thing write music on its own?"

"That's the problem," he said, thoughtfully puffing on his pipe. "It's a thing. It can't think, you have to train it to think."

"How would you even begin to do that?" I asked.

"You work from the simple to the complex. I'd start with a program that would make sense out of something that I already understood, like 'trig' functions. A function is something you feed into the program and watch what comes out the other end. In this case, you'd be looking for it to spit out a 'trig' table."

One of Ben's training programs was so successful that most of it is still in use today; interestingly, it is not a computer program but is a primary training guide for volunteers. This manual is filled with simple 'do's' and 'don'ts'.

Remembering what Ben had said about input and output, I asked, "Is this how you train volunteers? You plug in these 'do's' and 'don'ts' and watch what comes out the other end?"

"Of course," he answered, "you start with the simple and move to the complex. For example, there is the rule: 'do not carry anything out of the institution that you did not bring in'. It's a simple rule that applies to residents and staff, as well as volunteers. You teach them to crawl with the 'do's' and 'don'ts'. Then you teach them to walk and hope that eventually they can function responsibly in their job."

"How in the world do you get them on their feet and walking?"

"You teach them that they have a built-in alarm system. They need to be in touch with it."

"How so?"

"Go back to the rule of not carrying out something on behalf of an inmate. It could be something as simple as a resident asking a staff member or volunteer to carry out a letter to a dying mother. If you feel uncomfortable about it, then it's setting off an alarm. There is nothing wrong with a letter going out to a dying mother, but it may not be a letter to a dying mother. The alarm calls for 'stepping back' from the situation. This moment enables a person to evaluate the alarm to see where to go with it. All these alarms call on imagination to get someone up on their feet and running. You just hope that imagination doesn't lead someone in the wrong direction."

I saw men and women come to work at prison every day. Many of them shared their personal concerns with me. Their personal and psychological problems make them vulnerable to manipulation. Their most pressing concern could be anything from money to loneliness. Inmates know how to press these buttons. Lonely women have helped seriously dangerous inmates escape. Correctional officers bring in contraband for quick cash. Volunteers, unmindful of their role as 'caregiver,' sometimes cross the line. In so doing, they may not be violating a rule, but they do become enablers.

I looked forward to visiting with Ben in the early afternoon. He remarked that he knew the sound of my footsteps when I walked into the building. I looked forward to the smell of his pipe before entering the office.

One afternoon I had been held up at checkpoint. I watched a young correctional officer making the attempt to bring in alcohol in a Coke can. Rosco Clayton, our internal affairs person, came and took the officer away. Arriving at the office, I asked Ben, "What happened to the officer's alarm system?"

Shaking his head, he said, "I don't know. Maybe he had the volume turned down."

It was always on my mind but, for some reason, I was afraid to ask Ben my most pressing question: "How in the world does a rocket scientist turn Christian?" The time came when I popped that very question to him.

Ben's literal words were, "You take on His story." That's what the former rocket scientist did. I imagined Ben putting on a coat of many colors. Like any coat, it needs cleaning from time to time. It's lasting. You can count on it. It works. It works something like the 'trig' functions that Ben mentioned feeding into a computer. But unlike feeding 'trig' functions into a computer, a person feeds on His Words. With

13

practice one is up and running. You can trust what's going to come out the other end.

Ben died a few years back. The last time I saw him happened to be at a covered-dish supper. Feeling the urgency to say thanks, I pulled him aside. I thanked him for taking me in and giving me the opportunity for a ministry beyond the local church.

It was much more than a job beyond the local church. I felt at home. The seed was cast on fertile soil, the timing was right and so was the place, on the mark. Or, was it on the mark? Ironically and literally, my mother's one wish for me was not to go to prison. Nevertheless, I had come to a more abundant life where, as a chaplain, I could find joy in serving the Body of God in a prison environment.

As mentioned, one of our chaplains, Amos Wilson, thought of Ben as having the best analytical mind of anyone he had ever known. Along with that, Ben had imagination. The former rocket scientist took on the story of Christ! What can I say? "With rocket science and imagination comes 'wonderous being'."

Often, I am reminded of the images that Ben communicated. On the one hand, they were images of detachment: "Let it go. Put it on Mars. Step back." On the other hand, they were images to help me crawl, then walk, and finally run. Taking on the greatest story ever told can get anyone up and running.

Ben was a major milestone at an important turning point in my life. As I look back, I see so many who have been a blessing for me including residents, volunteers and staff members. What more can I say? My mentor used rocket fuel; I breathed pure oxygen!

RHODES SCHOLAR OR ROAD SCHOLAR

Working the evening hours gave me the opportunity to get acquainted with active volunteers and make rounds in the housing units. One of the first inmates that I met resided in housing unit 5. I came to learn that Harris had been recently reassigned to that housing unit. He had come off maximum-security where inmates are locked down 23 hours a day. While on the yard, I watched Harris practice martial arts moves with tremendous focus, forming a lasting image in my mind.

During count, I passed in a circle around the cells, occasionally speaking to an inmate on the other side of a heavy door. Looking through a narrow window in the door, I passed by Harris' cell and saw him reading. Surrounded by books, Harris seemed as focused on reading as he had been on the martial arts routine. When count cleared, the doors were popped open. I moseyed back over to his cell and introduced myself. Then, standing at the threshold of his cell, I noticed the books he had been reading, the Bible, and next to it, Plato's *Republic*. I also glanced at other books on his shelf: law books, the Bhagavad-Gita, books on meditation, psychology and political science. Harris rose from his bunk

16

and respectfully addressed me, "Thanks for stopping by, Chaplain." Pointing to his ID he said, "I'm Harris Hatfield."

"I see you're in pretty good company, Jesus and Socrates."

"Just trying to let time serve me, Chaplain. It's hard on a man to serve time." Abruptly I heard: "I dream of being a Rhodes Scholar." I felt like a pin-ball machine that had just been knocked almost off tilt. How, I wondered, did this guy come up with that? "You look surprised, Chaplain." I nodded in the affirmative. He continued. "Let me clarify myself. What's the best way to have time at your feet in this place? You have to take on a dream, a realistic dream!" Hatfield smiled and suddenly broke into a laugh. Not knowing where he was coming from or whether he was trying to be humorous, how could I help but laugh along with him.

"Chaplain, may I ask you a question?"

"Sure. Shoot."

"Can you spell Rhodes Scholar for me?"

I pronounced the title and then spelled the words: "Rhodes Scholar, RHODES SCHOLAR."

"No, Chaplain. Not in here. How could being a Rhodes Scholar in prison be realistic? It's not! In prison, being a 'ROAD SCHOLAR' is a realistic dream. I am a road scholar now and throughout time. I'm not putting it off. I'm living my dream...in the now...and that is existential!"

I laughed. "That makes you an existential road scholar."

"Right on, Chaplain, right on!" We were all hoots.

"What about you, Chaplain? You're new on the job. Why are you here? If you're like most of this lot, you're here to do eight and hit the gate. That's doing hard time, Chaplain. If you want to make it to retirement, you've got to have a realistic dream, like being a Road Scholar. How is time going to serve you in a place like this?"

"Woody Allen," I remarked to Harris, "said that ninety percent of life is just showing up. Why don't you show up in my office, say one evening out of the week, and we'll carry on a conversation. We'll explore what it means to become a road scholar."

When Harris first appeared at my office door, I glimpsed a youthful spirit with an openness to learn and a kind of innocence without the wrappings of dogma. It was like the ring of a bell. I heard 'youth' and 'truth' in the same ring.

I knew how to spell Rhodes Scholar and that Bill Clinton and Kris Kristofferson had been so chosen. I knew that these scholars studied at Oxford, but that was about it.

Harris had taken notes from a prison encyclopedia. The scholarship, established in 1902, was the result of a trust set up in honor of Cecil J. Rhodes, the organization's founder. Harris wasn't concerned about the organization's history but he did mention that Rhodes' wealth was tainted with the blood of South Africans who were exploited by him. Harris' focus was on the qualifications for the scholarship: high academic achievement, high moral character and the potential for leadership in whatever field the scholar chooses to pursue. These qualifications represent a commitment to others and the common good.

Harris said, "Although I will not become a member of this prestigious group, I choose to overcome my own stained history by pursuing and practicing virtue. Such is the purpose of the Rhodes Scholar and, in my case, a road scholar."

Eventually, Harris would share with me the story of how he had come to prison. He and one of his cronies murdered the owner of a gaming facility—an arcade—that catered to youth. Upon arriving at prison, Harris was young, small, and vulnerable to being picked on. He could have chosen a 'big daddy' or a gang for protection, but he didn't. He didn't want to adhere to the unwritten code of prison caste. If a person does not affiliate socially with this system of stronger over the weaker, the inmate will be intimidated and possibly killed. Harris did not want to conform to this code; he wanted to cast an image of intimidation, but he paid the price for it.

Harris was ready when a gang made the attempt to strong-arm him. They sent out one of their young members to bully Harris into submission. Harris struck first. While the

18

Bully was stretched out on a weight bench, Harris plunged a shank through his heart killing him. The young man had only one week left on his sentence. What was he thinking? He wasn't thinking; he was following the mindlessness of a herd.

Harris would not conform to the 'thought-adjuster' of any gang. The threat of being violated stood as his 'thought-adjuster'. Now other inmates and gang members knew not to draw too close. Other inmates, who had not witnessed his violence, would see him as an outsider. They would later remark to me, "He's a little off, Chaplain."

Many years later, I spoke with his mother on the phone. She said, "Of all my children, I would never have expected Harris to be the child who went to prison. Harris went to church and never gave us any trouble." I was not surprised when she told me this.

Often, Harris and I would have supper together in the dining hall. Sometimes, our discourse was during a walk around the ball field. On one of those occasions, Harris told me that coming to prison caused him to think long and hard about why he had committed murder. His way of taking responsibility for what he had done was to look at the influences and circumstances that led to his crime, one that he had committed with another person.

He explained, "I don't blame my charge partner; I blame myself for getting in that situation. That I can understand. Later, I chose to defend myself from the threats of a man at Turney Center. I was afraid for my life. I took responsibility for my life by taking a life. I was in a quandary. After the incident, I was locked down for a very long time. This was a no-win situation.

"Harris, let me tell you a story about conformity. It is a no-win situation on which you can meditate. Have you heard the 'Parable of Procrustes' Bed'?"

"No, Chaplain, I haven't."

"There is an ancient story that tells of travelers making their way north to Athens, the center of democracy and philosophy. On the way, they stop off at the Inn of Procrustes. Procrustes invites travelers to sleep in a magic bed. Here is the paradox. On the one hand, it is a bed that fits all travelers. On the other hand, the bed fits no one at all. It is also a metaphorical bed, a bed of conformity.

In the Middle Ages there was a literal bed of torture referred to as the bed of Procrustes. This rack served as a kind of 'thought adjuster' for those whose minds were not attuned to the dogma of the church or any other dogma that failed authority. Persons placed in the bed are either stretched to fit it or they are cut down in order to match the size of the bed. The metaphor becomes very real when folks are dragged to the rack for their unwillingness to conform to the mentality of a mob or a tyrant. It is more likely that a victim will willingly and blindly lay down in the bed of Procrustes as did the young man at Turney Center who took his turn on the weight bench in order to fit in with his gang."

Harris did meditate on the story. We met many times and discussed the parable.

"That story would have been a good introduction to Plato's *Republic* and the gospel," said Harris. "When one enters Athens, one is surrounded and tempted by the language of the herd, likewise when one enters Jerusalem. Mobs do not murder Rhodes Scholars; they murder road scholars. That said, I believe that Socrates had a partial answer: to engage in dialogue. The Socratic method keeps the conversation going."

Harris paused, then continued. "Jesus had His answer: 'To love one another.' Love is privileged over discourse. Socrates never could stand the mob; he willingly drank hemlock and gladly left this world. Jesus did not put blame on the throng that gathered and shouted for his execution. He said that no group or individual had control over his destiny, only the Father in heaven. He forgave the mob and agonized in the Garden of Gethsemane."

"You're right," I said. "Herd mentality is a vicious cycle of conflict and vindication. That's where we all are, lying in the bed of Procrustes, in a never-ending cycle of fear. How we stand up against tyranny is no easy choice. Unlike Socrates, Jesus reached out to common people and taught them to discern right from wrong. You can own your thoughts; I can own mine. We can join in discourse without putting one another on a rack. Words can 'become flesh,' bringing us more fully into the Kingdom of God."

"Yes," replied Harris, "But I hope that you are not discounting Socrates. He saw the problem. Man is 'not the measure of all things' nor does he have complete control over his destiny. Socrates did make a choice. He chose death. He chose the inevitable. He did not conform to the crowd. He simply laid down and died.

Harris continued, "The irony of it was that Socrates was the greatest sophist of all. This Greek philosopher's intention was not to practice rhetoric for gain or talking to delight in his own eloquence or merely winning an argument for a profit. This scholar in bare feet set me on the road and got me on the prowl toward virtue."

"Chaplain, I saw that there are tricksters out there and they can set you on a path to either heaven or hell. The greatest trickster is yourself. Have you ever run into a 'nobody' who led you down an unexpected path and afterwards you woke up and realized you'd been trashed? I did, and here I am. I agonize over that choice every day. Now, what about you, Chaplain; how did you wind up in prison? Which scholar set you on your path? I'll bet it wasn't a Rhodes Scholar!"

"I'll bet you're right, Harris. I'm looking for bare feet or sandals." We chuckled.

I would never have imagined it, but my friendship with Harris has lasted almost three decades. We later met again at Riverbend. At the time, I learned that Harris had become a devout Catholic. He regularly went to Mass with our Catholic deacon and was consistent in the practice of a devotional life. Even so, he was still considered an outlier by many of his peers.

When I was about to retire, Harris was coming up for parole. Several inmates from the Christian community came up to me and said, "That guy is crazy."

"How so?" I asked.

"He talks to himself on the ball field. He has paranoid thoughts, Chaplain."

These inmates talked among themselves and to one of our volunteer chaplains, Jerry Nail. "He's not right. He'll never pass the psych' exam." Jerry didn't believe a word of it. Jerry told me, "He might be different but he's not crazy."

I confronted Harris. "What's this about your talking to yourself on the ball field?"

Harris smiled and pulled out his rosary beads. "I trust that my prayers will be heard and I will leave this place. I know there are Christian brothers who think I'm paranoid."

A person charged with murder does not get released from prison without a psychological exam. Harris took the exam and was deemed sane.

In 2012 Harris came up for parole. No one can make parole without a suitable release plan, which would include a place to stay, a job and a mentor.

In twenty-one years, I had only endorsed two other inmates at their parole hearing, and Harris would be the third one. In addition, Harris' family drove from Texas to speak on his behalf. He had community support from his faith group as well as from several of our volunteers. He had a place to stay and a job at a transition program known as Building Lives. Harris decided to stick with the program for a period of one year. I arranged to be his mentor.

Tim Gregath, the program director of Building Lives, agreed that I would spend one day a week with Harris. I picked him up, as I recall, on Tuesdays.

At first, this involved the nuts and bolts of transition: seeing a doctor, a dentist, seeing about eye glasses, shopping, and later getting a driver's license. With these things under our belts, I gave Harris a job and paid him for it. Harris helped me complete the interior of a two-story cabin that I had spent the previous five years working on.

Shortly before leaving the transition center, a cousin offered Harris a place to stay in the town of Spring Hill, not too far from our home. During that time, Harris found a girlfriend---a registered nurse who worked around weekends in a nursing home. Her days off were Tuesday, Wednesday and Thursday. I thought for sure that this would be a roadblock for Harris. I assumed he'd be laid up with her on her days off and not come to work. I was wrong. When he found out that she had an issue with drugs, he dropped her like a hot potato. I was shocked. He never missed a day of work.

We enjoyed seeing the all-poplar interior come together---the ceiling, the stairs, the cabinets and the floors. Harris hooked his phone to a set of miniature speakers, and we worked to the sounds of Roy Orbison.

During lunch, we'd be sitting amidst construction debris chewing the cud. One day, Harris remarked, "I can't believe what's happening. After all these years, you and I are here, covered with sawdust, listening to this incredible music and eating baloney sandwiches."

"After all these years, I would never have imagined it either," I paused and then asked, "Do you remember once wanting to be a road scholar?"

"Yes, I do, Chaplain." Harris smiled and shook his head. "We went on and on about that, what I'd call stretching a gnat's behind over a telephone pole."

"Harris," I asked, "Do you remember when I got stumped by one of your road scholar questions?"

"What question?"

"I don't remember, but I thought you might remember."

Harris blurted out, "Chaplain, I stumped you all the time. I can't remember which stump you're talking about."

"How in the world did we ever get on the 'road scholar' kick?" I asked.

Harris replied, "I actually met an inmate who wanted to be a Rhodes Scholar. He believed in the importance of names and associated it with one's destiny. He reasoned that farting in public would evoke a name for that person, 'gasman'. That man avoided taking on a prison name. He considered these names frozen forms that served no function. I don't remember this guy's real name, but he did refer to himself as a road scholar, something akin to a road warrior.

23

He gave me his copy of the *Republic* and said that it would lead me forward to Jesus."

Harris paused and then continued, "I had a favorite parable in the *Republic*, 'The Ship of State'. My understanding of it kept me away from the wrong person or crowd in prison. There's no difference between a prison gang and a gang in the House of Representatives or the United States Senate. You must diagnose a mob or a tyrant when you see one, like recognizing your grandmother."

"Chaplain, imagine a ship of state adrift on the high sea, no one behind the helm. Imagine the war that goes on among the crew to take charge of the helm. Why would anyone have reason to believe that the navigator could lead them safely to shore when he is looking up at the stars? A mob would throw the navigator to the sharks. They want to take charge, so they never transcend their self-interest long enough to find out where they are or where they are headed."

I chuckled.

"Are you laughing, Chaplain?"

"No, I'm thinking about what you said, Harris. Speaking of a ship adrift with no one behind the helm is what I thought when you met the nurse that could have become your girlfriend. Harris, you showed focus. You might make it in the free world."

"Might make it! Come on, Chaplain! I'm a road scholar! Don't think that I'm adrift. Don't think that I can't recognize something like the bed of Procrustes! I see another bed, beyond that torture rack!"

"Ouch!" I exclaimed. We laughed.

Harris went on, "There is a bed of self-discovery; it is the bed of 'know-thyself.' If you discover the bed that transcends self-interest, you can lay down and sleep like a baby. I look to the Navigator to set my course toward wisdom."

Eventually, I drove Harris back to Texas where he settled down with his mother and father, brothers and sister. He started a construction/handy-man business, bought some land and is constructing a cabin to live in. He stays busy and has a girlfriend who works as a teacher. Harris lives an ordinary life and attends Mass. Who could possibly recognize him as a road scholar?

CAN PEOPLE CHOOSE HOW THEY CROSS OVER? HOW ABOUT PREACHING YOUR OWN FUNERAL?

William Meadows died on the 4th of July 2011. His wife, Sherry, asked me to do the funeral. I arrived at the Harpeth Hills Funeral Home about 10:30 AM on Friday, July 8th. Just before coming in the front door of the funeral home, I noticed a crowd had gathered. I did a double take when I saw one young lady who resembled Sherry.

Right before the funeral, this young lady approached me and remarked, "You thought that I was Sherry. I'm her cousin." She knew that I'd be doing the service and asked if I had any prison stories.

Everyone in prison has a story. Most of these stories are about suffering and hopelessness; one story looks like the next and the characters never change. Someone gets done in and someone gets even. Prison is a Ferris wheel of conflict and vindication.

What about a story where someone gets off that Ferris wheel of incarceration into a sequence of events without any reasonable human explanation? What about stepping off that Ferris wheel into a twilight-zone where all that remains is a glimpse of hope? What more can you offer in the face of

27

death? When a loved-one is taken away, all that is left is faith and hope.

I began the service with an invocation, the obituary and a prayer. After the opening hymn and before reading scripture, I informed the group that I had a prison story. "I'm going to pull a story out of the hat and you'll wonder, 'Where in the world did that come from'? The story does take place in a prison, Turney Center. The last time I talked with William, we discussed this story."

In the mid-nineties I served as chaplain at the Turney Center Industrial Prison and Farm. I had just bought a laptop computer. On a Saturday I carried it down to the high security housing unit to make my rounds. After visiting inmates, I stopped off to visit my friend, Harold Weatherford, the unit counselor who would be supervising visitation. I wanted to show him this new 'toy'.

In addition to his being a prison counselor, Harold served as a Baptist minister in a nearby church. At the time, Harold told me about a sermon that he planned to preach the next day entitled, *I'm Glad I'm Not a Golden Hawk.* It was about the restoration of an old Studebaker that turned out to be a flop. The outcome of the visit was that Harold dictated the sermon to me and I typed it on my new laptop. Sometime later, I went back to the unit and gave Harold a copy of his sermon.

On one occasion, around October of 1996, Harold told me about an unusual event: One of his minister friends dropped dead while preaching a sermon. In fact, he dropped dead behind the pulpit. Harold thought that there was no better way to go. Harold told me, "That's exactly the way I want to go out, preaching."

On Sunday November 17, 1996, nurse Cindy Mallard called me from the prison clinic. She'd just received word that Harold Weatherford had died of a massive heart attack while preaching that day. Harold's wife, Diana, asked if I'd speak at the funeral. She told me the events that surrounded Harold's death. He moved to the rear of the church during his sermon, looked to the front, declared that he saw Christ coming, ran forward and dropped dead.

There were lots of people at Harold's funeral. I delivered the sermon that Harold had dictated to me several months earlier: *I'm Glad I'm Not a Golden Hawk*. Harold went out the way he wanted, preaching. You might even say that he preached his own funeral.

At William's funeral, I read several of his poems. His devotion, in these poems, was to Jesus Christ, his friends, his family and, most of all, Sherry his wife. I told the group that I had never preached to or moralized with William. He had put a roof on a new cabin out back, and he and I put the siding on in the fall of the following year. I baptized William and performed his wedding with Sherry.

The last time he visited me, he had worries over the difficulty of getting work in a depressed market. He admitted having problems with his drinking and, occasionally, being on the outs with Sherry. We sat down together in the empty house out back (with the dog lying beside us) and had a heart-to-heart talk.

Being led, not so much by thought, as by the Spirit, I considered it important to fortify his faith and began to recount experiences that embrace a life of faith. I told him of Cecil Johnson's execution at Riverbend. In the face of death, all Cecil wanted was for his family and friends to have faith. In the end, Cecil embodied just that. William also declared the same faith at his baptism.

So why did I describe the events leading to Harold Weatherford's death at Williams funeral? Because William had heard the story and because it affirmed the faith of Harold Weatherford. In the face of death, the story points beyond itself and gives hope. Faith is what takes hold of hope. We all need to hear this; we are not alone, and death is swallowed up in a great victory.

A hearse carrying William's coffin was drawn by a Harley Davidson motorcycle. At the graveside, I shared with the congregation what I had seen. "When I stopped to turn left and drive up the hill to William's grave, I noticed a grave marker with a name on it written in bold letters. The name read Wertherford, spelled 'Wertherford' rather than 'Weatherford'." As I looked out into the crowd of people, I saw astonished expressions on their faces. Surely, the presence of God was in this place.

CONCLUDING SECTION FROM HAROLD WEATHERFORD'S FINAL SERMON:

I'M GLAD I'M NOT A GOLDEN HAWK

If you or I were an antique car buff and spotted a Golden Hawk rusting away, we'd likely have a vision of what it cost to restore. We'd purchase it and roll up our sleeves and go to work. What work we couldn't do ourselves; we'd have a professional do—someone whom we can trust. Just as the antique car buff is allowed to make a purchase for the Golden Hawk, so do we have to allow ourselves to be purchased by God. Just as the antique buff allows the professional mechanic or body and fender person to work on his treasure, so do we have to allow God to come into our lives and work on us.

How is God working in your life? Do you have a spare tire hanging over your belt? Maybe the lights are a little dim in your eyes? What kind of things have you been looking at lately? How about your radiator, is it blowing steam all the time? How about that old radio in the dash? What kind of music are you listening to? Maybe a fuse is burned out and you aren't listening to anything or all you're receiving is static? What about the interior; how does it smell? Does it smell like a brewery? How thick has the nicotine built up on the glass

32

and on the seat covers? The old and the new, the past and the present, what was, what is and what can be—that's the Golden Hawk. Even so, no one wants to be a Golden Hawk sitting in the junk yard rusting away. But just as the Golden Hawk can be redeemed, so can we find redemption through Christ Jesus. "Therefore, if anyone is in Christ, he is a new creation, old things have passed away; behold all things have become new" (II Cor. 5:17). The decision to follow Christ out of the junk yard of life and into the kingdom of heaven is up to you. Christ offers his love freely to all of us; it is up to each of us to answer His call. "And the Spirit and the bride says, Come!" (Rev. 22:17). I'm glad I'm not a Golden Hawk because I've been restored through Christ Jesus. How about you? Amen.

My Walk with Jesus

I walk with Jesus every day,
I can feel him at my side.
When I pray, I hear his words,
They sometimes make me sigh.

I talk with him a lot these days,
Since my life's been saved.
Waiting for everlasting life,
When the Lord takes me away.

I'll be with him someday soon,
I know for this is true.
He's waiting there with open arms,
For me and for you.

I love the feeling that I get,
When I pray to him each night.
How he has blessed my every wish,
By making things just right.

He said all I need is faith,
Believe and it will be.
Put my trust and love in Him,
Said it will set me free.

Written By: William Meadows
2/21/2006

The Free World

Since I have been free from prison,
My life has been really swell.
I try to focus on my Lord,
To save my soul from hell.

My life has really changed so much,
Since I let Jesus have his way.
O know the Lord knows what's best for me,
Each morning as I pray.

I try to do the best I can,
By walking in God's Word.
But the way things are this day and time,
His Word is seldom heard.

I give my testimony in God's House,
To people that want to hear.
How Jesus has entered into my life,
And the devil I no longer fear.

I hope someday my poems are published,
And God's Words prevail,
The words I write are from God above,
And friends like Jerry Nail.

Written By: William Meadows
9/03/2009

A MOCK EXECUTION

Today was the day that I carried out the role of prisoner in a mock execution by lethal injection. I walked into the visiting gallery about 12:45 PM where I met the last victim practiced on, and a person who I'd never met before. This stranger was the medical person who injects the needle into the veins of the victim. When these two learned that I would be today's condemned man, the state employee told me I'd better empty my bladder before going through the ordeal. She confessed having wet in her pants two weeks before. After the saline solution had been injected into her veins, they had to wait five minutes before pronouncing the prisoner dead and letting her get off the gurney. She couldn't wait, and the procedure had to be carried out. She went home dressed in the attire that the condemned prisoner will be wearing at the time of execution.

At 1:00 PM the execution team began to gather in the execution area which is behind the visitation area. The Warden was present when I walked into the actual execution room. The atmosphere was serious, but friendly.

The Warden took me behind the execution chamber and unlocked a door leading into a small room. This room is the area where the lethal chemicals are injected into the condemned prisoner. In this room I saw two bags of saline solution hanging from a stand sitting on a narrow bench.

There was a small square cut in the concrete block which opened into the execution room; the opening, as I recall, had a metal flap with slits which allowed the plastic lines to reach out to where the victim would be strapped on a gurney. On the bench were seven large syringes filled with the solution. I was told that in the event of a real execution, one of these syringes would be filled with a solution which would put the victim to sleep, another would stop the breathing and a third would stop the heart. The other liquid-filled syringes would be used to clean the line.

After addressing his team in the execution room, the Warden ordered everyone to take their places. I walked back to the control room in the death watch area, entered a restroom, and emptied my bladder. I then took my place in the first of four cells in the death watch zone. Earlier, the Warden had pointed out the cell that would be used for an upcoming execution. I heard the burgundy iron bars slam shut behind me. With elbows on knee and hands folded, I sat on the mattress-covered bunk and waited. In that wait I prayed for those condemned souls who might one day follow in this sad drama; I also prayed for forgiveness and a depth of understanding and compassion for all involved in this process.

The most startling part of the event was when the Warden marched into the death watch area with a line of about four or five correctional officers. He crossed through the threshold of an outer gate and approached my cell. I looked up from the bunk.

"It's time," he said. "Is there anything you would like to say before we take you in?"

"Yes, I'd like prayer," I said.

"Well, you can say a prayer," said the warden.

"I would like for my minister to pray," I replied.

Since there was no minister present, the warden had previously agreed to act that part. He said a short prayer. My mind was racing, and I do not remember the exact words, but the prayer came across as sincere and fitting. The warden asked that God have mercy and open his arms to receive me. At this point a correctional officer stepped up to the bars and

38

exclaimed, "Please step forward and extend your hands through the bars."

I did as instructed and heard the command: "Now, place your hands together."

My wrists were then bound with a thick plastic strap and the taper of the strap was cut with wire cutters.

"Now step back and place your knees on the bunk and your hands against the wall."

I did as instructed, then waited. I heard the door slide open. Two officers suddenly held me firmly under each of my arms. I heard and felt my ankles being shackled. Then they cuffed my wrists. A thick heavy leather belt was strapped around my waist; it had a silver ring in the front of it. The hand cuffs were then attached to it and I was stood up on my feet where another shackle was attached to the waist belt and the shackles on my legs. I got the sense that I had just been hog-tied.

The officers continued to hold me firmly in their grip---still, two officers on each side, hugging me and holding my arms. They shuffled me outside the cell, through the adjacent iron gate, to the death gurney that had been rolled into the area. By the side of the gurney, I could see down the passageway into the death chamber. In an instant one officer lifted my legs while two others held me firmly by the arms. After being placed face up on the gurney, several straps were secured across my body from the ankles to the chest. My ankles were then belted down and I was quickly rolled down the corridor and toward the terminal destination.

The gurney is finally placed beside that opening in the wall where the lethal injection tubes are hanging in visible sight. There is a narrow reflecting one-way mirror-window beside that opening. Whoever is on the other side---the inside of that room---can see out, but whoever is in the death chamber cannot see in. It is at this point that my own personal subjectivity has transformed into extreme objectivity. For psychological preservation I can no longer give myself over in imagination to death. I tell myself that the event is only a rehearsal.

39

As best as I can remember, the shackles are removed; the leather waist belt is unbuckled and slipped out from under my body. The plastic wrist band is snipped loose with the same familiar pair of wire cutters. I notice that the handles are red. The body straps are tightened, and two padded arm extensions are attached to the gurney. My arms are then placed on these extensions and strapped down at the wrists. My body is now ready for the insertion of two needles, one in each arm. At this point, two plastic conducting tubes are attached to the needles; all of this is secured with tape.

With the exception of the warden and the deputy warden, I recall the room being cleared. The warden picks up a phone on the wall and dials. Someone on the other end answers and the warden speaks.

"Are there any stays of execution?" There is a pause. "All right," he says and hangs up.

The warden signals the deputy warden who opens the blinds to the large window of the witness room. This room is to my right and about fifteen feet away. There is no one present in the room at this time. I watch as the warden slowly approaches the gurney and asks, "Do you have any final statement to make?"

"Yes," I reply.

The warden nods for me to speak.

"I want you all to know that I hold no hatred, bitterness or animosity. I ask God for the forgiveness of my sins. I also want the staff to know that, although I oppose capital punishment, God's love is available to all of us. I want each and every one of you here to know that I stand by you all. I am always available to you; I do this because of God's love and because I am your chaplain."

There was a short pause after these final words. The warden acknowledges the statement, glances at his reflection in the one-way mirror-window, and declares, "Proceed."

Within seconds I feel solution entering a major vein in my left arm, the arm closest to that opening in the wall. The system running into my right arm vein is merely a backup. It takes maybe two to three minutes for all the chemicals to be pumped into my body. By this time the condemned man would be beyond sleep and his respiration and heartbeat would have been arrested. There is a five-minute wait and someone enters who feels my pulse at the right carotid artery. They announce that I have expired at 1:54 PM. The warden draws a curtain beside the gurney. The deputy warden closes the blinds draped over the window of the witness room. I am told by the warden that the coroner will then come in and pronounce the real victim dead. I also learn that there is body bag under the victim and it will be used to bag the body for removal from the institution.

The needles are carefully removed from my veins and the wounds are bandaged. The straps are unbuckled and so are the leather restraints that hold my wrists and ankles. I arise, like Lazarus, step off the gurney onto the tile floor and walk away.

Why am I personally opposed to capital punishment? As a chaplain, I began working with the men on death row over ten years ago. I care for these men and would rather see my work restored rather than eradicated. From a theological point of view, I see Christ as one who both teaches and demonstrates a 'way of being' that is radically non-contentious. He evokes a moral response that is contrary to people intentionally destroying one another.

Being opposed to capital punishment, why would I voluntarily submit to playing the role of a condemned man in a mock execution? God's love is present with all of those who participate in this sad drama. I choose to participate with both inmates and staff because I am their chaplain. I see it as a ministry of Presence where God's love transcends the bounds of this human predicament.

The EXECUTION OF SEDLEY ALLEY

On Friday evening, June 23, 2006, Sedley Alley told me that he would be taken to death watch on Sunday morning (June 25, 2006). At the time, Sedley recounted a dream. He also handed me two papers that he had recently written. The first paper is entitled "Being on Death Watch!" It is intended simply to inform the reader what it is like to be on death watch. The second paper is entitled "Purpose in Life."

Sedley began recounting his dream by telling me that he was arguing with God over the current situation. He said, "It's not like I was asking God for a sign; I was just asking to receive His side of the conversation."

"Finally," he continued, "I cut the lights out, laid down and closed my eyes. I suddenly saw this beautiful blue sky and it was filled with angels as far back as the eye could see. They were from different races and various walks of life; some had wings, and some didn't. Many of them had robes down to their ankles and three of them wore expensive looking three-piece Armani suits and alligator shoes. Although I could see no baskets, these angels appeared to be reaching into baskets for flower petals and scattering them about. One angel came by and scattered petals across the side of my face. It startled me because, for a moment, I thought that it might be a spider crawling on my face. It was so realistic that I quickly brushed my face with my hand. I could not hear

43

anything or smell anything. My experience was heavenly, and peaceful. I slept soundly all night long."

I thought it odd that Sedley would tell me that he could not smell anything in the dream and asked him why he thought that detail to be important. He simply said that he could neither hear nor smell anything in the dream. I didn't say anything, but it occurred to me that he might have expected to smell the flower petals. It was obviously a comforting dream, and Sedley believed the angels were preparing the way for the coming of a King. In this case, the king is Christ and the transition is for all humankind.

"When the end comes," Sedley said, "the transition will be like the difference between night and day." Sedley thought that whatever comes to pass will not be recognized through the lens of our present-day culture.

When I arrived on death watch Sunday afternoon, the staff had assigned Sedley a cell two cells down from Paul Reid. As I sat across the bars from Sedley, we began discussing his statement on "Purpose in Life." From the 'get go' there would be two major themes that we would regularly discuss throughout the death watch period. These general topics covered purpose and communication. Sedley believed that God has a purpose and plan for all of us and he said that we should love one another as God loved us and have forgiveness. He hoped that he would continue to be around to spread this good news but would accept moving on if that be in God's plan.

Sedley, in a way, was a very private person. As far as I am aware, he never spoke with the media and asked me not to speak to them about him. He had reservations on how effectively he could communicate with others. He said things like, "I don't know how to get people to listen to me. I have had these thoughts and feelings most of my life; I just don't know how to express them. The difference now is that depression comes from not being able to express myself the way I would like to." But, in the end, Sedley desired to reach out to others with his thoughts and words. Sedley asked me to deliver his two papers to Bill Stevens, who is the Unit 2 reporter for the prison newspaper, the *Maximum Times*. I asked Sedley, "If the opportunity came about, would you give permission for your two papers to be published in an article or book that supported the abolition of capital punishment?" Sedley agreed.

For almost all of Sedley's life, he remained haunted by the dramatic statement of his childhood Sunday school teacher, Ms. Sheila Doolin. "You, Sedley Alley, God has a plan for you!" Finally, Sedley took a stand when he states: "I looked at myself and where I am and what I could do from in here. Not much — but it came to me that maybe I am supposed to talk. I can't see that plan being anything other than getting a message out, talking."

Although talking about important issues challenged Sedley, he had a 'gift to gab' and plenty of curiosity and imagination to go with it. In 1990 His Holiness the Dalai Lama visited a small group of inmates on death row. Sedley began asking questions about consciousness and meditation. The Dalai Lama told his associate to visit with the group while he took Sedley aside for a private discussion.

In 1998 I began Tuesday evening visits to Sedley and several others on death row. Some of what we did was to listen to and discuss Art Bell radio interviews that covered all kinds of out-of-the-way topics that might go from ghosts to hardcore physics. During the first day of my visit on death watch, the topic surfaced of Coral Castle down in Homestead, Florida. On Monday, I brought a sermon about the building of a castle out of coral that weighted hundreds of tons. A man five-foot tall weighing 100 pounds built the castle — a mystery to everyone. At this point, Sedley put me on the spot. "I think that you ought to communicate that message — you ought to have it published."

I told Sedley I had the same syndrome he had. "I don't know how to get people to listen to me; they don't want to hear that way-out stuff."

Sedley and I argued a bit over this issue of being heard. I told Sedley that I was 'preached out' and asked him if he really wanted to hear more. Apparently, he did and he asked me to bring another sermon the next day. It was at this point that we both realized that we shared similar wounds from trying to communicate the deepest part of ourselves.

In Sedley's talk with God before his dream experience, he was asking to receive God's side of the conversation. In our discussion, as well as in Sedley's purpose statement, he says, "God really does talk to us; it's just that we don't always realize that it's Him doing the talking, and we don't always understand exactly what He is saying. I feel this has more to do with us than Him."

Right before Sedley went on death watch the first time, he received a letter from an inmate who wanted to know why God didn't seem to be listening to the misery of all the inmates on maximum-security. If Sedley had to go, he asked if Sedley would have a talk with God about his concern. Sedley and I talked about the 'communion of saints'. We agreed. We could use all the help that we could get on this side.

Considering Sedley's request to hear from God, I brought a sermon entitled "The Way of the Desert." The Three Temptations of Christ deals with moving away from the world and others; it is a posture of detachment where the believer waits in silent attendance for personal revelation and transformation. After sharing the message, I felt a bit exasperated. The message begins by recounting a practical joke played on a college student. Someone placed a dead skunk in the back of his car. Thinking he would rid the car of the smell, the student drove the car several hundred miles. The corny image of the skunk runs throughout the entire sermon.

"Sedley," I went on, "I just don't get it. You, of all people, know about vindictive justice. We know that it stinks. Why would I bring you something that we've already talked about? Do you suppose that there could be some other purpose in this message at a time like this?" Neither Sedley nor I could grasp any deeper meaning, although the meaning would become clear later. We weren't thinking about it at the time, but the sermon merely directed the hearer to wait in silent attendance.

On many occasions, Sedley would tell me that his main concern was for his kids and those around him who were providing care and support. He seemed to be holding up pretty well on the surface, but it must have been very difficult. Sedley kept an upset stomach and told me that he had been passing blood. When I asked him how it felt to be in this situation, he said that he couldn't describe it. If he made it back to the unit, he'd tell me then. Sedley asked if I would pray for God to provide strength. We prayed and around 10:00 p.m. we had communion. Inmate Paul Reid took communion with us.

There was a stay in place for Sedley up to the end. When the officers began to move Paul Reid to another location and prison officials appeared on the walk, Sedley remarked, "It's over." The phone rang and Sedley got the message from his attorney. I could hear him thanking them for all that they had done. He hung up the phone, turned to me and said, "They've vacated the stay."

The warden stood in front of the cell. Words were exchanged. Sedley and I held both hands through the prison bars. I prayed and, together, we both said the Lord's Prayer. I then went to be with Sedley's family. Just before his execution, the warden asked if he had any last words. His last words were to his children: "I love you and stay strong." Before he died, he thanked and blessed me.

The following day, Paul Reid's execution was still in question. The men in Unit 6 were still on lock-down. Later that afternoon I walked over to Unit 6 to check with my office clerk, David Phipps. Many men in Unit 6 had expressed deep concern over this execution and had asked me to tell Sedley that they were in constant prayer for him. David had me take a seat in his cell. A few remarks were exchanged about the previous day and the early morning. David gave me a serious look and said, "I had an epiphany." I was all ears.

David continued, "This cell is the first one ducted into from the air conditioning system. About two o'clock last night a skunk or two got into the trash outside. Skunk spray was so bad in this cell that our eyes watered."

"My God," I replied! "That was at the time they executed Sedley. You won't believe this, but I brought Sedley a skunk sermon and we were both wondering if it had some deeper meaning or purpose."

I hurried back to my office and retrieved a copy of the message and brought it back to David. As we recounted the events that had come to pass, David's witness bore witness to my witness and my witness bore witness to his witness. We remembered God's Word, the Upper Room, and the walk to Emmaus. Our eyes were suddenly opened, and we witnessed the Spirit of our Comforter.

There were other skunk sightings around the compound... and smells. Bill Stevens, the reporter on death row, whose cell looks down on death watch, spotted a "huge skunk prowling in the area around 12:30 AM."

At this point in time and in this country, a state-sanctioned execution reflects the consciousness of a collective which puts out life and light. It is a message that tells us that certain lives cannot be salvaged or redeemed. This is the height of imaginative bankruptcy.

Through Christ, however, there is hope. Jesus said, "Let not your hearts be troubled. I will pray the Father, and he will give you another Counselor, to be with you forever, even the Spirit of truth, whom the world cannot receive, because it neither sees him nor knows him; you know him, for he dwells with you, and will be in you."

BEING ON DEATH WATCH
By Sedley Alley

Being on death watch is totally different from how I thought it would be. You hear rumors and what's supposed to be personal accounts of the experience and you develop ideas about how you think something is going to be. Well, I am going to try to give an honest accounting of what my experience was from start to finish.

Don't pack anything expecting to be able to keep it in your cell on death watch. I do think that you should pack everything up, especially things that you want to have access to while you're there. These things include your tobacco and matches, stuff to read, and some commissary like candy bars, chips, soap, shampoo and a comb, the sort of stuff you need every day. Pack a personal bag, but don't expect to keep anything in your cell on death watch. Everything you have is taken from your cell in the housing unit. You can't keep anything in the cell with you, but you have access to it whenever you want it, your personal or daily items. Perhaps I was lucky having gone on a Sunday. All my property stayed with me. It was all inventoried and gone through right down to the smallest things and property lists are filled out and put in each bag of property just in case.

The first few hours are the worst, because you're not sure how things are going to go, and you don't know for sure

50

what you're going to be allowed to have access to. It is made clear that you can keep some items close by to use while you're there but for the most part your stuff is packed up and you can't keep getting stuff out of it. I would imagine that if you really felt that you needed something, and it could be found easily then you could have it kept with your tobacco and other stuff. I kept my Bible close and a magazine to read along with the daily stuff.

I know that rumors run wild about how things are up there, but I am here to set the record straight on how things are. You can watch TV or listen to the radio or do nothing at all, the choice is yours. They have a TV in the walk just outside your cell and they have a radio for you to listen to. They change the channels for you. If you want a cigarette, they get it for you and light it. You can smoke all you want to. They have coffee up there and anytime I wanted a cup someone would get it for me. Everything you drink is gotten for you in small Styrofoam cups, which you have to give back when you're finished with it.

Everything is written down about how you're doing and what you're doing. Trust me, there is no privacy at all. You are not bothered if you don't want to be, but you are watched very closely. You shower and use the bathroom right out in the open. They don't stand and watch every little wipe, but they are right there just outside the bars keeping track of what you're doing.

Every time you leave your cell, for any reason, you are strip searched and given a complete change of clothes. Everything is changed, even your underwear, T-shirt and socks.

On all visits, attorney and family are non-contact. I was told that I could have one contact visit with my family that last day but you are in full restraints during the contact visit and at least one officer stays in the room with you and your family. Times may vary a bit but my family visits were from 9 AM to 11 AM and 1 PM to 3 PM each day. Attorneys can visit whenever they need to but all their visits are non-contact. You have access to a phone pretty much all day and night. You

51

have a more or less direct line that your attorneys can use to call you or you can call them when you feel you need to.

The thing that struck me the most was the total lack of privacy. You are never alone. They don't sit and stare at you but you're never totally out of their sight. Of course, we all know why that is. They don't want you doing anything to yourself. I have to say, even though you're watched the entire time, you are able to sit and not be bothered if you don't want to be bothered. You can be alone in this regard if you want to be.

I know that things will be a bit different for each person who has to go up there. Everybody is different, and their situation is different. There are two 12 hour shifts and everybody was respectful and polite. My family was treated with respect, and nobody said or did anything that bothered me or my family personally. I mean, being on death watch is bad enough and the personnel realize that. Everyone acted with polite respect and professionalism, and for myself and my family I thank them for that.

I pray that no one has to go through that again but chances are someone will eventually have to go up there and deal with it. The main thing I found to be true is that no matter what, never give up and don't let it get the better of you. Remember that there are a lot of people praying for each of us and prayer does make a difference.

PURPOSE IN LIFE

By Sedley Alley

What is my purpose in life? Why am I here? What am I supposed to do with or in my life? Questions, I would imagine, everyone has asked at least once in their lives. I have asked these questions several times myself, especially after the experience with my Sunday school teacher, Shelia Doolin, in the church that Sunday evening a very long time ago.

She screamed and shouted, "You Sedley Alley, God Has A Plan for You!"

I just about screamed myself, only out of fear not divine prompting. She ran back to the front of the church and continued praying. I left the church in a hurry that evening, but I kept thinking about what she said and what it meant. After I thought about it for a while, I let it go and finally stopped thinking about it.

In the last 10 years or so the memory of that experience has come back to me, and I have been thinking about what it could've meant. I looked at myself and where I am and what I could do from in here. Not much, but it came to me that maybe I am supposed to talk. I just can't see that plan being anything other than getting out a message by talking. I'm not good at much else other than talking. I do love to talk, and

54

I've been told that I was born with the gift of gab. I was also born with a kind of wonderment about things. I want to know how things work and why things are the way they are. I want to understand things. The most powerful thing I can think of is God and His purpose in life for people, not just me but others as well. I have given it all a lot of prayerful thought and I think that we are getting it all wrong. We're missing the point of what He was/is trying to tell us.

So, the next question is, "How to go about telling the world that they've gotten it all wrong and this is what He really meant?" I may have been born with a gift of gab, but I don't know how to get people to listen to me, especially those that aren't inclined to listen to me from the get-go or those who want to listen to someone else.

It came to me that maybe, just maybe, my purpose is to say, "Hey You People, Can't You Get the Point? When He Said Love Each Other, That's What He Really Does Mean. Love one Another As He loves You." Christ said it better than I ever could. A few examples are *Matthew* 5:38-48, 7:1-2 and 7:12. Then there's *John* 8:7 but of course you could read all the words in red in your Bible. If you actually did that for yourself, you would get a whole different picture of what it really means to be a Christian.

Personally, I feel that the conservative stance is an indefensible position by true Christian standards. The liberal stance is more in line with the way Christ lived His life and is the way we should live our lives. Being more Christ-like is the actual meaning of being a Christian.

Physical, emotional and spiritual pain kept me from being able to write things down like I wanted to for most of my life. Though I have had these thoughts and feelings most of my life, I just didn't know how to express them. I am now 50 years old and I spent 35 of those years getting stoned and drunk and dealing with intense physical and emotional and spiritual pain. The pain and illnesses I had as a child are what led me to drugs and drinking. The drugs and drinking led to a very deep depression that I still haven't fully shook. The difference now is that depression comes from not being able to express myself the way I would like to.

I have always felt that being a liberal, the way the word is used today, is the right way to be. I know in today's world being truly liberal can mean being taken advantage of but most people can tell when they are being used by others. I feel that it's better to err on the side of doing the right thing rather than on the side of doing the wrong thing.

I find it difficult to reconcile the conservative way with being a Christian. The two just don't mix. Taking away from the neediest to give to the better off is wrong. Killing anyone is wrong, although I personally feel that self-defense is acceptable by man's standards but not by God's standards. The balancing act between the two, I feel, would be to only kill when you are being attacked by someone who intends to kill you. Once the attack is over, the killing should stop on either side of the fight. The death penalty doesn't stop killing after the incident. The death penalty will keep killing years, even decades, after the battle is over. People enjoy doing it.

I've been locked up since 1985 and have been on death row since March 1987. Everyone that I've met here is no different than anyone I met out there before I got locked up. For the most part, they're good hard-working people that let drugs and /or alcohol take control of their lives. Some are what could be called 'insane' if they weren't on death row but, since they're here, they're considered sane enough to kill. Some are truly innocent of the crimes they're here for, some did it but not for the reasons or in it the way that the state said they did. Some actually did what they're here for. But even for those few that are truly guilty, the death penalty is just plain wrong.

Christ said, "Judge not lest ye be judged." We have only one example of what Christ would actually do if confronted with a death penalty case and he chose life. You can put all the twists and turns on it you want but the fact still remains that given an actual death penalty case, Christ chose life not death. The woman caught in adultery was that case. Jesus didn't require anything of her, but that she sin no more.

The USA is way behind the curve on this issue, right back there with countries that we say are Third World and terrorist supporters, countries like Iran, North Korea, China, just to name a few. Even Russia did away with the death penalty several years ago. Of the First World countries, the USA stands virtually alone, if not totally alone, in killing its own people with a death penalty. In fact, most countries try to rehabilitate their prison inmates. The USA doesn't rehabilitate anyone. They just warehouse people. Prisons have become a huge business in this country. Keeping people locked up and killing some of them makes a lot of people a lot of money.

My experience on death row has been, overall, a positive one. I've gotten to meet a lot of really good people. I have also met some that aren't so good. Getting to meet these people is a blessing just the same. I have learned what it means to truly be a friend and have friends. My walk with Christ has become much more real to me and a lot more personal. I still ask a lot of seemingly dumb questions of God, but I feel that I have been given a lot of really good answers along the way.

I don't know for sure if my fate is to die here or live to be 110. Whichever it is, I know that I have been forgiven for the sins that I have committed, and I have forgiven those few that have wronged me along the way. I know in my heart that we will all meet in heaven and have some really nice long talks about everything that has happened here on earth. I feel that God really does talk to us. It's just that we don't always realize that it's Him doing the talking, and we don't always understand exactly what He is saying. That has more to do with us than with Him.

When I pray, I can talk about and ask about some pretty unusual stuff, but I feel that God always answers even if I don't always know what He is saying to me. Some things come through clear as a bell. Even though I am here on death row, I am truly blessed.

I know that to some that sounds weird but it's true. My life has been blessed in more ways than I could ever hope to express, starting with my two children. Every experience I have had over the 50 years of my life has led me to this point and, even though I am here on death row, I feel that overall my life has been a good life.

I don't know if I will have enough time to finish writing all that I feel I need to write but what I am writing I feel really needs to be said. God has a plan in mind and that plan will be fulfilled. The only question that remains is, "Are we going to be willing participants in that plan or are we going to go kicking and screaming into its fulfillment?"

Personally, I want to be a willing participant in God's plan and help as many others as possible realize that they, too, can and should be willing participants in God's plan. We all have to walk the path that is set before us, and the thing I want to let everybody know is that all those different paths lead to God and heaven. We are all saved by Grace and God freely gives that forgiveness and salvation to all.

I feel that God can and does work miracles in our lives. All we need to do is pray that we will be able to recognize them. I pray that I will be allowed to remain here on earth and be allowed to continue to write and share what I feel I need to share but, if that is not God's will, then I accept that, too. While I am here and can share with others, I feel that the two main things that need to be shared are: love one another as we are loved by God and, freely and openly, forgive one another as God forgives us.

I feel that people learn to hate. Love is a natural thing for us but we have to be willing to learn and share it. Treat others the way you would like to be treated is an old idea but a true one.

Continue to pray for whatever you feel you should pray for and don't forget to remember others in those prayers. Be open to what God is trying to let you know. Love one another and forgive others. Be willing to accept God's forgiveness for whatever you may have done and you will be fine in this life and in the life to come.

UNINTENDED CONSEQUENCES: THE DEATH PENALTY'S IMPACT ON CORRECTIONAL STAFF

I'm on my phone the other day. I ask it, "botched executions?" Up came cases where the victim is reported to be conscious during the execution. I saw pictures of botched electrocutions where people caught fire and were disfigured. They even have 'stats' on botched executions.

I told my friend Jim about the race to execute 11 men in Arkansas last year because the drugs being used were about to expire. With his compassionate position, he said, "They need to put those executions on hold until we can be more humane."

But there is another side to the story. One online comment went like this, "A slow death would suit me fine. That's what he dealt out to his victim. Justice has been served. This gives me closure."

There's a third position that I've seen employees take. As I recall there was a high employee turnover rate at Riverbend. Several employees told me that they were simply showing up for the medical benefits. Some said, "I'm doing my eight; I'm following policy; I'm hitting the gate." There have been some third shift workers dismissed for sleeping on the job. For these people, coming to work is just a ritual, merely a means to making a living. Policy becomes a set of rules that gives assurance of keeping their job. I think that it's safe to say that these people are not mindfully present to what they call their vocation. Their response to an execution is: silence or indifference.

A state-sanctioned execution is also a ritual act. A team will practice this procedure on each other. They call this ritual "band practice." Practice forms habits. We learn that, with practice, action becomes 'second nature'. When an act becomes second nature, one does not have to think about it. That's the down side or negative consequence of a human being involved in a ritual act---you don't have to think about what you are doing, much less what you're about as a human being. One winds up "just doing his job."

The problem begins when we don't stop to realize that we live in a world of self and others. We reveal our humanity when we can imagine, and act on the fact, that another person has thoughts and emotions just like we do. How we treat other people has a consequence. How an organization treats its employees has a consequence.

Not too many years ago, Harmon Wray and Richard Goode came to Riverbend with Vanderbilt divinity students to teach restorative justice. Their goal was not so much to teach the class 'what to think' but 'how to think' about crime and punishment. If you have enough people thinking about restoration rather than retribution, you have a paradigm shift.

The law liberated slaves at the time of the Civil War, but it did not change the dominant narrative. You had Jim Crow laws passed in the South. The Clan grew in numbers. Blacks were lynched by the hundreds. Racism still exists in America, particularly in the South.

You have those who support the dominant narrative, those who are indifferent, and those who want the model to change. Nothing will change until enough people change how they think about crime and punishment and stand up for what they believe.

I have seen an execution take its toll on correctional staff: psychologically and emotionally. Sedley Alley was shackled for his final contact visit with his two children. They were hanging onto him and crying their eyes out. It was very upsetting for the correctional officer looking in on that scene, including myself. Right before Sedley Alley's execution, Sedley was so upset that he couldn't move to the cell door. The officer in charge went beyond standard protocol when he had two officers go into the cell. The OIC said, "Be gentle with him." Later, that same officer told me, "I hated to see that. Sedley and I go way back." That officer connected to Sedley in a very human way. This event made an indelible impression on him as well as on me.

There have been urban legends coming out of Riverbend's involvement in executions. An employee went back to death watch to do wiring in the ceiling of the death chamber. He fell and hung upside down for quite some time before help came. The employee lost his sight. A pregnant nurse participated in an execution and later lost her baby.

Upon walking out of the institution following the execution of Sedley Alley, I stopped to chat briefly with a ranking officer. I knew that this person helped to carry out the execution. Having had previous conversations with this person, I suspected that he had administered the fatal injection. I remember him smoking a cigarette. There is the smell of skunk spray in the air. The officer connects the smell with the execution. He remarks, "That's strange." People know more than they can understand. Urban legends come about for a reason. People find a way of dealing with these surprise events.

The following day I found myself in the deputy warden's office where he expressed his shock at witnessing Sedley's two children crying. They were "carrying on and slinging snot on the glass partition" as they watched the state execute their father. I respect the deputy warden because, under all that prison veneer, he could feel something and showed it. He had no problem retiring a few years later.

If you want to change the dominant narrative, you must change the way people think. People who practice mindfulness are present in their relationships with others. They don't come to work to sleep through their shift. They don't come to work and sign up to participate in an execution because "it is their job." They don't use a scriptural passage or two to justify a killing. They come to work because they are fully human and believe that their voices and choices make a difference. They are awake! This change in one's disposition---how we treat each other---sets the tone for a movement from retributive to restorative justice.

A SKUNK, A SHOE and A BOOK: A REFLECTION ON SYCHRONICITY

"There are two ways to be fooled. One is to believe what isn't true; the other is to refuse to believe what is true."

Soren Kierkegaard

In the chapter, "The Execution of Sedley Alley," Sedley and I were discussing the death penalty. I brought in a sermon threaded with the image of a skunk. We connected this stink with execution. Later, prior to and during the execution, skunks were roaming the compound. Here we have two events. The first event is the sharing of our thoughts. The second happening is the actual materialization of skunks letting out their smell during the execution. Now, connect those two events and you have what the psychologist Carl Jung calls synchronicity.

It's also called a meaningful coincidence. What makes it an apparent coincidence is the fact that we were discussing the subject prior to the actual event of skunks appearing on the scene. If the event happened first, we might connect the stink to the matter of executing people, but it may not carry the same punch. Neither of these experiences are entirely congruent with how we ordinarily experience our world. It gives us pause.

Let me give you another example. Most mornings my wife, Sarah, and I drive down to the local community center, park the car, then jog or walk. One morning she was upset and needed to calm down. I tell her "that's why we're out for exercise, to help relieve tension." She walks a half mile and back. I jog a mile down the road and return. On the way out, I notice a pair of shoes and blue jeans lying in the ditch. At the time, it seems odd that someone would leave such items on the side of the road, in a ditch. Upon returning to the car, I find that Sarah has retrieved one of the shoes and is examining it. She draws my attention to the inside tongue of the shoe. It reads: "Clear the mind." I looked at Sarah and said, "If the shoe fits, wear it." This seemed so strange that I photographed the message in the shoe.

In the early eighties, I had taken a leave from ministry. Just before my return to the Tennessee Conference of the United Methodist Church, I had been reading some of the writings of the church fathers. I visited a book shop in Sarasota, Florida, in search of Thomas De Sales' *The Devout Life*. There had to have been several thousand books on the shelves in that shop. I went in three times looking for the book. On the third try, I stood across the checkout counter talking with the book-seller on the other side. As I was about to ask the man to order the book, I heard a noise coming from behind me. There was no one else in the store other than the clerk and myself. I turned and noticed that a book had fallen off the shelf. As I reached down to pick up the book, I somehow knew that it would be the book that I had been looking for, *The Devout Life*.

I don't imagine a devout Christian having a problem with such an experience. They would attribute it to the Holy Spirit, teaching, directing and bringing comfort. The clerk on the other side of the counter had an interesting reaction. When he saw that it was the book that I had been in search of, he held out his hands as if he were separating himself from something. He said, "It was just a coincidence." Astounded, I asked, "Yes, but how did that book fall off the shelf?"

In ancient times, the God Hermes, guide of souls, was viewed as being in charge of carrying both messages and mortals across boundaries. Jesus is a hermetic character. He has no "certain dwelling place;" he cannot be pinned down; he carries us across borders of the unexpected.

In the above three examples of synchronicity, messages appear and borders are crossed. Murder stinks when it crosses death. Clearing the mind changes an agitated mind to a quiet one. A book falling off the self with the message of living a devout life suggests doing just that, when I cross back into ministry. All of these incidences come as a surprise and with a punch. How can these surprises be understood or explained away?

I realize that one could read most anything into an unusual experience, but that's not a way out. These experiences certainly catch one's attention. Jennifer Skiff's delightful book entitled, *God Stories*, is filled with personal encounters of mysterious happenings.

There are psychologists and scientists like Carl Jung and Wolfgang Pauli who have speculations regarding synchronicity. These thinkers, and others like them, have associated synchronicity with the collective unconscious, quantum physics, an implicate order, a holographic universe, a noosphere, the I-Ching and Tao. As interesting as these theories are, they leave us scratching our heads.

One of the most interesting books on this subject is by David J. Hand entitled, *The Improbability Principal: Why Coincidences, Miracles, and Rare Events Happen Every Day.* Put very simply, statistics is the rationale behind these anomalous occurrences. A million to one odds against having the right lottery ticket will pop a winning ticket for someone. David Hand thinks that this way of thinking takes the mystery out of 'weird' experiences.

From the perspective of statistics and quantum physics, this is entirely possible. Does having a good statistical explanation for the unexpected explain away alternative explanations? Is it possible that we can't imagine what we don't know? Is there an underlying and mysterious order that cannot be ruled out by sound reasoning, quantum physics, or statistical analysis? These do not rule out other possible explanations yet to be discovered.

The notion of synchronicity is strongly associated with psychic content within a person's subjective experience. The easy problems of consciousness specify mechanisms that describe functions, like sight or hearing. The 'hard problem' of consciousness deals with the actual phenomenal experience. Neuroscientists and philosophers haven't solved the problem.

A synchronicity has its own unique intention coming from the individual observer, as well as shape and coloration of the senses. What I said to my wife was meant for her: "If the shoe fits wear it." The assumption does not refer to the feet of everyone. The actual shoe fits another person's foot. My wife's experience may impact her behavior. This apparent incongruity may set her course of action in a mindful direction. She may, in fact, act on the message and "clear her mind."

A breakthrough of the 'uncanny' resists a mechanistic explanation. In the case of psychic phenomena, the phenomena itself are put in question. Hence, synchronicity can be easily dismissed. If not, it presents itself as mystery because it is a mystery and often evokes a response from us.

The driving ideology behind an antiquated science is a materialistic explanation. It is no different from the outlook of the pre-Socratics who sought the origin of Being in stuff: earth, air, fire and water. Science takes 'stuff' and creates new and novel 'stuff' for our practical convenience and mutual self-destruction.

The philosopher Karl Popper calls this reductive perspective "promissory materialism." Promissory materialism offers notes for discoveries yet to be made. Parapsychologists are holding that promissory note. They are waiting for more evidence in order to establish credibility. Creationists, on the other hand, have cashed in that note with 'scientific evidence' that shores up their belief system.

Synchronicity is far beyond my understanding. Even so, as a believer, who walks by faith and not by sight, I have no problem taking on God's poetry---a skunk, a shoe and a book. Maybe there is a poetic nature of individual and collective consciousness, a unified field of music or harmony that penetrates our vast cosmos.

Synchronicities are said to be acausal. I don't believe that at all. God's creation has design. That said, I'm not cashing in on Popper's promissory note to shore up my belief system. I believe in creation by design simply through faith. Take prayer, for example. My daughter, Amy, right after having major surgery, prays to God for the right person to come into her life. She prays that the birthday of that person will be the same date of her prayer on July 31. That date will be a sign to her from God that she has met the right person.

Faith is the substance of things hoped for; the evidence of things not seen (Heb. 11:1). With respect to 'the substance of things hoped for' Amy met the right person. Robert is the answer to her prayer. He was, in fact, born on July 31, the evidence of things not seen.

Such an experience can impact one's belief system and behavior. I can't bring myself to believe that her experience was acausal. Amy made a connection. Her prayer was heard. The transfer of information cannot be measured out in probable events or coffee spoons with lumps of sugar and cream. These unusual experiences are gifts that suggest the surprise of a Living Kingdom breaking into the lived experience. These experiences can be a transforming moment in a person's life.

A SURPRISE REUNION!

"Then the Kingdom of Heaven will be like ten virgins, who took their lamps, and went out to meet the bridegroom. Five of them were foolish, and five were wise. Those who were foolish, when they took their lamps, took no oil with them, but the wise took oil in their vessels with their lamps.

Now while the bridegroom delayed, they all slumbered and slept. But at midnight there was a cry, 'Behold! The bridegroom is coming! Come out to meet him!' Then all those virgins arose and trimmed their lamps. The foolish said to the wise, 'Give us some of your oil, for our lamps are going out.'

But the wise answered, saying, 'What if there isn't enough for us and you? You go rather to those who sell and buy for yourselves.'

While they went away to buy, the bridegroom came, and those who were ready went in with him to the marriage feast, and the door was shut. Afterward the other virgins also came, saying, 'Lord, Lord, open to us.'

But he answered, 'Most assuredly I tell you, I don't know you.' Watch therefore, for you don't know the day nor the hour in which the Son of Man is coming." Mt. 25:1-13.

In the summer of 1999 I walked into a cigar store and made the acquaintance of a courteous and bright young clerk named Ben. In the course of our conversation, I learned that Ben was a student who would soon be graduating from Middle Tennessee State University with a Bachelor of Arts degree. When he told me that his major was philosophy, we connected with a common interest. I told Ben that I worked as a chaplain at the local maximum-security prison in Nashville and that I coordinated religious and volunteer activities. I also told him about having brought a philosophy class to inmates and how well it went over. I told Ben about the possibility of bringing philosophical and psychological insights to inmates who were locked down 23 hours a day by visiting them through the pie-flap in their cell door.

Ben had an interest in logic, but talked about existential concepts as well. He mentioned the work of Jean Paul Sartre, *Being and Nothingness,* and how it had influenced the direction of his life. I didn't know it at the time, but this book would come up again in the unfolding of the journey we would be taking together.

As our conversation proceeded, Ben expressed the importance of having Christian values. He envisioned giving back something to his community. He conveyed compassion for men in prison, especially those his own age who did not have the opportunities presented to him. He imagined philosophy as a way of liberating the human spirit. The prospect of being a volunteer and bringing philosophy to inmates immediately came alive in him. I wasted no time in taking Ben through volunteer training. He later came in to be fingerprinted and have his picture taken. The intake staff issued Ben an ID badge.

Ben thought of an innovative way to bring philosophy to inmates, a way that would make it easy to understand and discuss. Ben brought a novel about the history of philosophy---*Sophie's World.* He brought five or ten copies of these books out to the prison. I took him to housing unit 4, a unit where a small group of inmates would be able to meet in the visiting gallery. Some of the men knew about philosophy and were eager to begin. A couple of these men thought they were coming to a Bible study. They all stayed for the group and came back the following week. Upon making my weekly visit to unit 4, I found members of the group in lively discussion over the content of their new activity. Ben was excited over the insights that these men shared with the group.

The men in Ben's group were classified as 'close custody', meaning that they had recently been reclassified and were likely to be moved to another prison. After several weeks, Ben's group dropped to 2 or 3 members. Although staff stressed the need for group activities on the units and requested it, they did not or could not accommodate my requests to keep these men on the unit for the duration of this program. Late one afternoon, the officer in charge of the unit picked up the phone and called me over to speak with Ben. All the class members had been shipped, and Ben expressed pronounced disappointment.

I did not want to let Ben down. So, I asked myself, "How can we make this work?" I remembered a middle-aged man from housing unit 6, a minimum-security unit across from the chapel whose inmate residents are considered support staff. One of the inmates from unit 6, named Michael, had been coming over to my office to discuss his current readings in the philosophy of George Santayana. Our meetings had nothing to do with mentoring or being a part of some group activity.

Michael came across as being very well read in philosophy. I felt as if I were the one being tutored. Although Michael had not earned a degree in philosophy, he expressed plans to return to college and take up the major. After Michael's release from prison, he did return to college, MTSU, and earned a degree with a major in philosophy.

I asked Ben, "Would you mind meeting with an older guy who reads Santayana and who probably won't get shipped? We can call him to the chapel and you guys can meet in my office or in the chapel, whichever is open."

I recall Ben perking up to the idea. "Sure, let's do it."

We walked together over to housing unit 6 and entered the building. I addressed an officer on duty and asked for Michael to be brought out of a pod into the central area where we would be waiting to meet him. The officer walked into the pod and called out for Michael.

When Michael walked through the heavy pod door, he made a sudden stop and called out the name, "Ben." Ben heard his name called and turned to the pod door where Michael stood. I'm watching this dramatic moment. Ben's jaw literally dropped, his eyes bulged. Ben raised his arm and pointed in the direction of Michael, with his finger, and said, "That's the man who gave me the book that changed my life." Both guys were stunned.

Ten years earlier Michael had been living in a suburb with his wife. They had recently traveled to Europe with a troupe bringing drama and music. Michael linked this act with a performance of humor, satire, irony and creativity and talked as if their home were a salon of sorts, where artists would come and go with their creations. The couple often took in someone with no place to stay. One day, Ben appeared with a friend and met their host, Michael. Ben looked over Michael's collection of books and took one off the shelf, *Being and Nothingness* by Jean Paul Sartre. Michael lent Ben the book and Ben later returned it. It was the book that Ben claimed changed the direction of his life, the same book that he mentioned when we first met in the cigar store.

Indeed, this happening came across as an uncanny event unfolding in front of my eyes. What caught my attention was not the irony or peculiar circumstances taking place, but something that I needed to take in and claim for myself. In those moments, where one questions purpose and meaning, I ask myself, and I expect that we all ask ourselves, "What good am I to anyone? Does what I do really count? Personally, I wondered about having worth in a prison where so many abide, only to return.

It happened to be a transforming moment for me. I witnessed a young man, with conviction, point to an inmate, whom he had met ten years earlier and stated that a simple act of lending a book changed his life. And there stood the inmate, Michael, a prisoner, coming face-to-face with a human voice echoing from the past. "That's the man that gave me the book that changed my life."

And here is Ben, giving books to other young men in the hopes that this act will make a difference. Interestingly, I saw this occurrence coming from within Ben's own heart. He did not need external validation to act as he did. It revealed itself for what it was, a gift to those who were being held captive. It sent a message to me. "Have courage and stand firm under grace, knowing that you can walk by faith where the presence of love will inevitably let itself be known."

Michael was released from prison and attended Middle Tennessee State University where he earned a degree in philosophy. Life took him to other places. Michael returned to the Nashville area and we resumed our relationship. We worked together on a project building an octagonal yurt in a wooded area near our home. Neither time nor space can totally disentangle our lives. I'll never forget the phone call from Michael the Saturday evening before Cecil's Johnson's execution, but that's another story.

08/15/1999

REFLECTING ON A SURPRISE REUNION

Ben, Jerry and Michael

What I'd like to discuss is the day when you---Ben and Michael---met after ten years. It was dramatic to you guys; it appeared very dramatic to me. We can reflect on it phenomenologically, theologically, existentially, pathologically...Ben. [laugh] Ben, start off and let's reflect. What happened? What was the event that day, what did we talk about, how did you feel, etc.?

B. I remember that we were having a hard time with the other guys from unit four. Everybody backed out of the program or got transferred. We had to leave the unit because someone set their cell on fire. Remember that?

J. Yes, there was a lot of smoke in the pod.

B. We decided to go to unit 6. We got in there and you had them page Michael. As we were standing there, I heard my name called. I didn't exactly expect my name to be called; it was Michael. The moment struck me as extremely ironic, mainly because I had come out here with the intention to teach

77

philosophy, with the intention to use some of it, to foster, I suppose, an approach to decision-making. Not necessarily on telling people what decisions to make but being a bit more paranoid about how to make decisions, go through a little more contemplation and what not. And it is certainly ironic mainly because the first philosophical piece I ever read was Jean Paul Sartre's *Being and Nothingness*. The copy I got from Michael was when I was fifteen, about ten years ago. The irony overtook me; it was a bit much in the sense that I was unable to systematize it. I couldn't place it into a history. It was my own history, definitely something I didn't expect.

J.   When we left the unit, do you recall what we talked about?

B.   To be honest, I was a bit numb at the time. I was caught in my own head.

J.   ...Or maybe when you were leaving the institution?

B.   Yea, yea...there was a discussion on...I guess the best word would be synchronicity---change is not just one of those things that is completely random. Things all fit into some sort of purpose or plan. There is an intention behind the activity at hand, or some sort of purposiveness which, I suppose, none of us really had access to at the time. But you were the first to really have an intuition of it. A lot of me was still stuck in my head...I wasn't sure.

J.   But we did decide that we would reflect on it.

B.   Oh, definitely.

J.   That we would put it on the back-burner and...

B.   Let's not lose this moment...

J. ...and deal with it. You were dumbfounded. You were really, really struck by it. And, Mike, what about your experience? How did you feel? Describe what took place from your frame of reference?

M. Well, that was how long ago, five months ago? I was fresh from a revocation hearing. My parole had been revoked from having backed over a bicycle...having lost a couple of semesters in the process. So, when I saw Ben, the first thing that struck me was that this was a mockery of fate. [laugh] ...Of my fate because Ben is engaged in the activities that I had planned for myself and which were taken from me. Simultaneously, with that thought, I had not forgotten that Ben was one of the very few who had ever returned a book borrowed from me. I've lent thousands of books over the years, I'm sure. If someone shows an interest in something to read, especially if I've already read it, the opportunity should be made available. Ben had actually gone out and bought another copy because the other one got lost. He put a notation on the inside cover, thanking me for loaning the book which was exceptional.

J. So, he embarked on a career in philosophy after reading this book. [smile]

M. Right. [smile] Well, I had no idea that my loaning the book was of any great significance to anything, really. Here was just another person interested in a book. It was my practice to give these things away; I didn't expect it to come back. [turning to Ben] I was glad to see you; it was nice to see a familiar face because I was new here. There was a comfort there for me. I didn't know, couldn't imagine what you were there for. I thought that it was probably something to do with some internship from school.

J. It's ironic, the week before, Ben had bought books and taken a number of the books to men in unit 4 who got

79

transferred the following week. The idea that Ben is now giving away books is sort of interesting. [laugh]

M. Well, yea.

J. I've had some insight into this, but I'm going to hold back from my history. I was wondering if you guys have any insight---philosophical or theological and, if you do, what is it and can it be shared among us in a meaningful way?

B. I think the most overt thing to be noticed is that there's some sort of symbolism. If I were to read this in a novel, I would notice a continuous sort of symbol. I would notice that immediately. To be quite honest, when I received the book from Michael, it was very much: "You look interested, try this out." Unit 4 is the same sort of attitude: "You guys look interested, let's try this out." In fact, one of the guys, the bald-headed one, looked at me right before we started and said, "Hey, this is no religion stuff. I'm not interested in believing what you believe."

"I'm not telling you what to believe, I'm just showing you this, you can take from it what you want." I can only assume that was the same spirit behind *Being and Nothingness*. There was a bit more of a hammer punch by Sartre. He has to be very compelling to read him---at least, at the time you read him. Having recently been thinking about history and thinking about significance of events and things of that nature---and concepts like recurrence---I began to really start thinking about how recurrence centers itself and focuses itself around events we deem significant, and we deem these events in comparison to other events we've had before. The significance, which was flagged in irony, is mainly because of the similarity of what was going on at the time. Cloaked in this irony, it became that much brighter. It struck really hard. It was like, wow this is really weird! [laugh]

M. Otherworldly? [laugh]

B. I expected to have conversations like this with you, just not in this setting.

M. Right. I suppose from a certain theological take on the issue or from a synchronistic viewpoint you can see things. Of course, it's all about what you're seeing with. But the significance is something arbitrary, of greater or lesser degree. Let's take, for instance, what's going on with Mohammad.[2] I suppose because he's the freshest example or incidence of this imposition of significance on something that...escapes me. What could be that significant as far as the specific end of Ramadhan? Not being among that faith group myself, I can maintain a level of indifference. It is frustrating and I agree with you [turning to J.] from a legalistic standpoint. I'm repulsed by that. It seems almost anal retentive to me.

J. I'm personally informed by, not only my experience--- the concrete events that take place in my life---I mean, seeing you guys meet and seeing both your jaws drop had a big impact on me.

M. Did my jaw drop? [laugh]

J. Yea, you looked really startled to me. I know Ben was because he pointed. [J. points as B. did] He pointed like a dog or something---with his finger.

M. Instead of your nose. [turning to B. laughing]

J. And so, here's an event. I began to stew on it a bit. Ben was expressing some things about the faith to me at one point. Suddenly, my symbolic world came alive---that I use to make my way in the world, from a Christian point of view. The

---

1 Mohammad came into the office right before the verbatim. He came across obsessed about the precise close of Ramadhan. Those volunteers from the Middle East told us it was over. Mohammed's personal Eman from the West had not called with what Mohammad considered the final word.

thing that came to my mind was the "Parable of the Ten Virgins." Ben comes like a 'thief in the night.' In the parable, Jesus also comes unexpectedly. Surprise! You recognize Ben as the one who you set on a significant journey ten years earlier. Now, Ben is doing what you did, reaching out to young men. Significance is what changes our lives. There is reason to celebrate as in the parable. Who knows, ten years from now a guy could come up to Ben. Ben might not recognize him, or he might recognize him. The guy could say, "That's the guy that gave me the book that changed my life." What that said to me, using that parable, was striking. I hope in an existential way---in such a way that confirms my mission---to be very intentional about my ministry. When this symbolism came together with my experience, it was not just meaningful. It bordered on the mystical. To me, it's something that I can realistically share with other people. It was something like an ah-ha moment! The experience doesn't explain how it happened or necessarily why it happened, but I feel greatly benefited by having witnessed the event. I feel it has had a transforming effect on my life.

B. Indeed, I think that the three of us would probably be in agreement, saying that it wasn't the normal run-of-the-mill sort of moment. I don't think it's one of those things that gets washed away at the end of the night. There was some significance recognized. Something about crossing of paths. Being a sort of scientist [laugh], I tend to try find a proper explanation---to file and connect these things into a systematized manner, and what not. On a superficial level, there wasn't anything different about that moment that couldn't have been forgotten. In fact, I didn't forget it. That was one of the things that kept me really, really thinking. Mainly because there was something that I understood as significant, intersubjectively. We all shared the experience.

J. Ben, what do you think?

B. Indeed, every moment is pregnant with this sort of thing, whatever it may be.

M. Potentially.

B. Exactly. The difficulty in being able to do is keeping track of your own story. That involves stepping outside of yourself and looking back. That's kind of difficult to do, especially when you find it a bit repulsive that you are being or might be judged. Narratives sometimes carry judgment. The "Parable of the Ten Virgins" certainly calls consideration to those who can't stay awake or pay attention. The parable carries judgment; I'm put on trial and it calls for a response.

J. I look back at my life and see experiences like this where I've missed something. I guess, in that sense, I was not prepared or awake. I felt judged. What if one of those men in your group showed up ten years later and claimed that your book changed his life. Do you respond by saying, "So what?"

B. Oh, dear. [laugh]

J. "Oh, dear," was not your response when you reunited with Mike. This parable seems to give some significance to the events in our lives. What do you guys think?

M. Well, as I said earlier, I think it's the significance that you impart to an event that is important. In my spiritual days [laugh] I was much more attuned to that way of seeing, but I haven't been in a long time. Initially, my first thought was that there was some cruel mockery of fate. Seeing on another level other than just the concrete, I was able to recognize the coincidence of it. Being in prison and having gone through a boxing match, as it were, with administrations and the state and a few other more intimate personages, I suppose, I was a little gun shy. I was expecting blows from the Fates

83

themselves. It was a natural reflex for me. Here it comes again.

J. Getting beat up again?

M. I'm getting beaten again. It's a very self-contained way of seeing---maybe merges on a paranoid way of seeing. There's a flinching; after so many blows you just flinch, here comes something else. As it turns out, it's ignited the three of us. It has turned out to be a very beneficial event for me. I have managed to reacquaint with Ben. We were never bosom pals or anything, but we associated.

[interruption]

J. [Back after the interruption] We've said a lot. I'm curious about the language we use. I mentioned the "Parable of the Ten Virgins." Mike, you said that you had used this language before, but it didn't work. Did you say that?

M. What language?

B. In your more spiritual days.

M. Oh, sure---to see things in a more metaphysical fashion.

J. Okay. What's particularly metaphorical---I mean metaphysical---about the way I interpreted my experience? I mean, we all understand it, don't we?

B. Yea.

M. Sure. It's a view of the meaning of an event.

J. When you were going through your religious period, did people sit around and explain their experiences in light of the gospel? Were they doing what we're doing?

84

M. Oh, certainly, certainly.

J. Did it make sense?

M. To a degree. I think you can stretch a metaphor for miles. You can find scriptural analogies in everyday experiences from washing the dishes to what have you. In spiritual terms, people who have a belief system---a religious or theological belief---probably have more of a proclivity to view things that way. I'd mentioned to you the other night about seeing the guy attacked by butterflies at the rest area off the interstate. I don't suppose that you could call it spiritual, but it's more of a poetic mode of viewing, of seeing. It was an irony that was lost on my companion at the time but, as I mentioned to her, you have to appreciate the contradiction of a man attacked by butterflies in a rest area. They were yellow and sulfurous, and he was batting his arms about. It's unusual to see butterflies behaving in that manner anyway. There was turbulence there, in the rest area.

J. Maybe you saw that as a motif in your life at the time? You told me that you had gone to a state park and stayed in a cabin off in the woods to rest, have peace, but evidently you had to leave early.
[phone rings and we continue the conversation]

M. About significance---we're getting all these distractions and intrusions from people who have their own items of significance. The irony is here at the moment. People are knocking on windows, calling on phones, and they all have something important which may or may not be of that much significance to us.

J. But it's important to them.

M. It's important to them and it's like a badminton match, isn't it? They're hittin' em over to our court.

85

J.   We can see the same metaphor here, in this event, as you saw in the guy in the rest area that couldn't get any rest in the rest area. [laugh] It was a symbol of what was going on in your life---a metaphor for what was happening to you at the time.

M. Sure.   Butterflies   are   cosmopolitan,   harmless, innocuous creatures.

B.   [laugh] Just harmless creatures can be a blessing.

J.   The use of symbolic, mythical language is important to me. I think to some extent that it's rather arbitrary. When I see what took place between you guys and see how important it's been to Ben, in his life, I feel convicted. [another outside interruption and Jerry is waving Mohammad away from the window] Here we've got another distraction! It's happening again.

M. It's just butterflies. [all laugh]

J.   I feel convicted. I want to be very intentional about what I do.

B. I recognize a certain amount of arbitrariness on evaluating what we're doing at the moment. I use my criterion to judge through things that I think through my eyes. The strange thing, the weird thing, is that there is a point that merges the three narratives and gives us all access to the same thing.

J.   Yes, that's very good.

B. I think that's a symbol's strong point and weak point. A symbol means nothing or a symbol does not work if more than one person doesn't buy into it.

86

J.   Right. I think this might be what happens in religious experiences and statements about those experiences. Sometimes the statement makes sense, but a lot of the time people just seem to be stumped by: "God told me to do this; God told me to do that."

B.   I'll agree, yea, more often than not. That pushes me in the direction I was going. Sure, I can speak in this language and sure I can find a way to fully describe a lot of my experiences, but it's not that it's unnecessary to speak on a religious tone using the symbols of religion, parable, myth, poetry, and art. It's not that I find it unnecessary because a lot of things get lost without it. I find it just as necessary to be fluent in the other languages---mainly materialism, arranged materialism, which is grasping the world in an iron tight grip. It's one thing to be able to speak one language, and it's another thing to be able to find parallels and maybe create a translation.

J.   Maybe these different languages have their strengths and weaknesses?

B.   Indeed, but one thing that we can keep in mind is, when it all comes down to it, there is at least one overarching narrative that encompasses all of us. We can call that reality, if you want. Indeed, if Michael were to do something that would cross my path, it could dramatically change the parameters of my life. Say, if I were to leave my car on the interstate, some poor guy driving behind me is going to find a great deal of significance in my action. [all laugh] We all understand life well enough to know that anytime we walk into a crowd of women...[laughs]...there's going to be at least one individual whose narrative is going to ignite your narrative. The reason why our narratives intersect is because we all plant in the same ground or meadow.

J.   I appreciate it guys.

THE EXECUTION OF CECIL JOHNSON: THE PIGEON AND THE TITANS

Every Wednesday I go with two of our volunteers to visit a group of inmates on death row. Several weeks before Cecil's execution, I encountered him on this regular stop in the unit. Cecil had his apron on and was working in the kitchen area. We greeted each other, and I asked, "How are you doing?"

Without hesitation, he answered, "I'm doing fine!" He assured me that he was firmly standing on faith. Cecil adamantly insisted that I not be grim over his impending execution. He voiced concern over the 'negative' and 'gloomy' attitudes of those around him. When I came back on the unit the following week and saw Cecil, he repeated what he'd said the week before. I said to myself that I would take Cecil at his word. I certainly hoped that his faith was helping to get him through this ordeal. However, it occurred to me that he might be of the belief that his faith would somehow 'get him off the hook'.

After our Wednesday evening meeting on death row one of our volunteers, Jeannie Alexander, goes with me over to building 11 where she leads a group in centering prayer. One of the inmates in this group happens to be a maintenance worker over on death row. On several occasions this inmate, nicknamed Fuzzy, expressed a great deal of concern over

89

Cecil's faith, thinking that it was naïve. Fuzzy looks deadly serious and says to me, "Chaplain, I've told Cecil 'to face it'; they will execute you! Chaplain, you need to go have a talk with that man!"

I was a bit taken back by Fuzzy's observation. It was not my read on the matter. Nevertheless, I had once had the same thought: maybe Cecil is thinking that his faith will literally 'get him out of this execution.' The following week, I confronted Cecil over the possibility of an easy faith. "Regardless of what happens, have you put this matter in God's hands? Do you trust Him? Do you have His peace?" Although Cecil did not want to die, he assured me that the matter was in God's hands. That settled it for me.

On November 25th, one week before Cecil's execution, Jeannie and I were in my office preparing to walk to our weekly group on death row. Fuzzy happens to be in the area with us and again comments on Cecil's naive faith. Jeannie had also talked with Cecil on the unit and comments that this is not her read on the situation. As Jeannie and I walk out the door and start down the walk, we continue to discuss the issue of Cecil's faith. Suddenly, we are startled by a solid white pigeon that instantly takes to flight inches in front of us. We stepped back, and I see this pigeon swoop up into the air. Jeannie excitedly exclaims, "Did you see that pigeon?" I thought of the pigeon as a dove and said so. We remarked on this unique occurrence, an occurrence taking place at the same time we were discussing Cecil's faith.

When Jeannie and I arrived on death row, Cecil came out to our meeting. The recurring theme in this saga appeared to be one of faith. Within myself, I kept asking: "What is authentic faith? What is the faith that truly moves mountains?" As in the Three Temptations of Christ, authentic faith is certainly not the faith that tempts God.

This would be Jeannie's last visit with Cecil, and neither Jeannie nor I questioned Cecil's faith. Although we were dumbfounded by our recent brush with a white pigeon, it was not brought up in our discussion that evening. It was Cecil who brought up the topic of faith, and he read a poem that he had written entitled "Blessed."

Shortly after our meeting with Cecil and others, Jeannie and I were back in building 11 where we began our regularly scheduled prayer meeting. Jeannie read *Luke* 21:12-19, and we all sat for 20 minutes in silence. I sat there wondering what I could possibly say to a condemned man that would make any difference or that would be of redeeming value? The words in the reading that caught my attention were the lines, "...for I myself will give you a wisdom in speaking...". At Jeannie's request I took a copy of this reading to Cecil the following Sunday after he had been taken to death watch.

Three days, before an execution takes place, the condemned man is brought off housing unit 2, and placed on watch until he is moved to the execution chamber a short distance away. Advent, the 29th of November, marked the morning that Cecil was escorted to a death watch holding cell. I arrived at the institution about 12:30 that afternoon.

While passing through checkpoint, I crossed paths with Cecil's wife, Sarah, who had just visited Cecil. She appeared stressed. We began a conversation about her concerns. Cecil's major concern for Sarah consisted in her taking on a strong faith and having God's peace. We prayed together. Before leaving, I had an urge to tell her about the pigeon that flew by Jeannie and me as we discussed Cecil's faith. Sarah looked amazed and exclaimed, "Cecil loves pigeons and one saved his life!" What she meant to say was that in attempting to save a pigeon, Cecil almost got killed, but was miraculously spared.

Upon arriving at Cecil's cell, I recounted our pigeon experience as well as the recent discussion with his wife. "What's this about your trying to save a pigeon and almost being done in?" I asked.

Cecil began to tell his story with excitement. As a young boy, he loved pigeons. One day he and his brother spotted a white baby pigeon stranded in the overhang of a tall barn. He and his brother went into the barn and climbed to

The Execution of Cecil Johnson

the highest level, where Cecil went through an opening and climbed up to save this stranded bird. He grabbed the pigeon and, on the way, down, Cecil lost his grip and fell.

"I was saved!" he exclaimed. "My pants got caught on a large bolt sticking out of the barn." He gestured with his hands showing me how round and how long the thing was that protruded from the barn.

"What happened to the pigeon you were trying to save?" I asked.

"On the way down, I threw the pigeon to my brother. We raised it. For a long time it would follow me around."

Cecil and I reflected on how these things had come to pass. When we prayed together, Cecil asked God that his witness to others would strengthen their trust and faith in Jesus Christ. He asked me to look up *Titus* 1:2. As I looked into the scripture, he said, "God doesn't lie!"

I came back to death watch later that day, just in time to watch football with Cecil. The Tennessee Titans were playing the Arizona Cardinals. After the first quarter, Cecil's attorney came for a visit and I left for home. I arrived home just in time to get the last quarter of the game. As I watched the game, I couldn't help make an analogy between the 'redemption' of the Titans and the redemption of Cecil. Early in the season the Titans had lost six straight games and were beginning to make a comeback with a fresh quarterback. In the last two or so minutes of the game, the Titans were behind and needed a touchdown to win. They were on or near their own five-yard line. In a breathtaking series of plays and first downs, they made it just short of a touchdown. On fourth down and time running out, they scored. I couldn't believe it!

The next day, Cecil and I were overcome with excitement and wonder; we were laughing and carrying on.

"Cecil!" I exclaimed. "I was thinking about you during that whole game, especially during that last drive and the score by the Titans."

Smiling, Cecil said, "I knew someone was watching that game and having the same thoughts that came to me. I told my wife this; I was sure of it!"

"Well, Cecil, it's all dazzling."

"I learned something, Chaplain."

"What did you learn, Cecil?"

"It's like this, Chaplain; the Titans had fourth and long on three different occasions as they made that final drive. On each of those fourth downs, I had faith that they would make it and they did. When it came down to the last play of the game, with six seconds left, I lost my faith. I just didn't believe they'd make it...but they did!"

I commented, "You lost faith and it was restored and fortified." I paused. "Let me ask you a question, Cecil. If it's fourth down, six seconds remaining, the ball is snapped, the clock is running, and time runs out before the end of play, is the game officially over?"

Cecil came alive with excitement. "Time can run out, but the game is not over until the end of the play!"

Giving Cecil a serious look, I said, "I, too, learned something from this experience, something quite mind-boggling." Cecil became all ears. "I was just like you during the final drive, totally absorbed in the game and making the analogy between you and the Titans. Will they all come out winners? Suddenly, the phone rings and my wife answers it. She answers the phone right about the time the Titans start their drive down the field. The Titans get a first down, I'm hanging on a thread, and she brings me the phone: "It's Michael, calling from Washington.""

Michael is the former inmate who was in the earlier story, "A Surprise Reunion." I didn't want to be rude and put Michael off; I didn't want to say that I'd call him right back, because a relationship is more important than a football game. So, there is all this static going on. I'm not able to concentrate either on Michael or the football game very well. Michael does say that he's planning a trip to Oregon. I hear negativity coming from him. He's complaining about having a record and having to go through a background check even for a job at McDonald's. He had other gripes and misgivings: marriage, getting into graduate school, becoming a professor

The Execution of Cecil Johnson

or lawyer. His attitude was clearly 'poor me'. At this point, I can see that it's near the last play of the game.

Suddenly, Michael makes this startling remark. "...and I don't need Jesus."

Had I actually proposed, or in some way, mentioned Jesus to Michael? I don't think so! Considering where my thoughts were, this totally took me off guard. To say the least, it was like being hit with a bat on the head. I was stunned--- stopped in my tracks. What could I say to a philosophy major who lacked the awareness of where my head was at the time? As I sat there, with a stupid look on my face, I heard cheers and then the sound of the announcer: "TOUCH DOWN, TITANS!"

When the time of the execution arrived, I was with Cecil the last two hours of his life. His concern was for his wife and friends. His hope never changed. He wanted a stronger faith for those left behind. He assured me that, when the clock stopped, his eyes would be on Jesus. The warden came and told Cecil that "it was time." His attorney was present and told Cecil that the Supreme Court had turned down the final appeal at 12:30 AM. We prayed. I left the area, and Cecil went to meet his Savior.

01/04/ 2010

BLESSED

By Cecil Johnson

I'm not blessed by the wonders of
the world, but by the faith and trust
I have in my Lord, Jesus Christ.

My destiny is not written by Man's
understanding and my life is not detailed
By the road you see before me.

I'm not blessed by man's praises or by
what he sees in me, but by the love
of my Lord, Jesus Christ.

My life is more than my smile, more than
the clothes I wear, for I walk not for
man's happiness, but for my Lord's desire.

I'm not blessed by material gain from the
world, but by the peace, love and strength
that comes through trusting in my Lord,
Jesus Christ.

My faith does not come from what man can
create, nor from what man can take away,
but from His heavenly love.

I'm not blessed by the things that my eyes
can see, but by the spirit of His Love,
by the revelation of the Word of our Lord,
Jesus Christ.

CAPTAIN TO THE BRIDGE:
ENTERING THE NARRATIVE OF THE OTHER

"Recognize what is in your sight, and that which is hidden from you will become plain to you."

The Gospel of Thomas

The idea that reality is, to some extent, a social construction is not new. That's what the Greeks were all about, 'man being the measure of all things.' The pipe puffing chaplain was right when he talked about folks "making it up as they went through life" and winding up in prison. Socrates' answer to his interlocutors was to serve the highest Good. In Christianity, Christ incarnates the standard of the Good. The Old and New Testaments speak as if we are co-creators with almighty God. That said, we live in an intersubjective world and we're called to get along with others, as in "love your neighbor." That's why Christians take on the story of Christ. They enter the narrative of Jesus and bridge the gap between self and others. The whole experience can be, at times, startling. It can also be a dirty business, as depicted in the event described in this account.

One of the best stories concerning entering the narrative of another person came from Chaplain Brian Darnell, now the Director of Religious and Volunteer Services for the Tennessee Department of Correction. His story is an example of a healing fiction.

At the time, Brian was working as a psychiatric chaplain at the Lois DeBerry Special Needs Facility in Nashville. He gets a phone call from the psychiatrist on duty who says, "We need your help. Can you come over?"

The chaplain scurries across the compound to the psychiatric ward. Upon entering the ward, the first thing the chaplain sees is a cell extraction team, fully suited. A ranking officer, wearing a face shield, is bent over peering through the pie-flap of a cell door. He is struggling to coax a resident to come out and take a shower. The ranking officer looks up and comments, "We don't want to make this difficult." The chaplain bends down, without a face shield, and peers into the cell. Suddenly, the chaplain is in a 'far-off country,' as in the pig pen of the prodigal son. He could not be any closer to stench and filth; it is the very reason the extraction team resists extraction: contamination.

Asphyxiated in a terrestrial moment, the chaplain discovers a resident having a celestial experience, a movement in height far beyond the 'summit of Everest.' Wallowing in his own feces, the resident is struggling against alien forces. He glances at the chaplain peering through the pie-flap and freezes. Suddenly, unexpectedly, the inmate calls out, "Captain to the bridge! Captain to the bridge!"

The chaplain retorts, "Bridge to the Captain!"

In the twinkling of an eye, the inmate acknowledges the bridge. The chaplain has connected and continues. "Dr. Spock has confirmed alien contamination. You are instructed to immediately proceed to the decontamination chamber!" The inmate rapidly picks himself up from the floor and swiftly steps toward the door. He extends his hands and wrists through the pie-flap in preparation for being handcuffed and taken to the shower.

The psychiatrist is in the wings, watching this drama unfold. Does she or anyone else in the wings yell out, "Eureka?" Apparently, not. And yet, there is something arresting, even numinous or funny, about the incident. The psychiatrist admonishes the chaplain. The chaplain is accused of entering the patient's psychosis and fostering his illness.

In fact, the chaplain made a connection by not assuming a clinical standpoint of distance. That is, the chaplain did not take on a 'white coat' viewpoint that detaches the clinician from the subject of treatment. The inmate resists interpretation; he seeks understanding, which includes a personal connection within the realm of his own subjective world view. He is not being understood. In that sense, he is in exile. The psychiatrist invited the chaplain over to help. The resident invited him in. "Captain to the bridge!"

"Bridge to the Captain!" They connect as subjects, not objects!

The clinical perspective is associated with a scientific world view. This scientific world view is what I would call *heuristic*. The Nobel Prize winning psychologist, Daniel Kahneman, states that "the technical definition of *heuristic* is a simple procedure that helps find adequate, though often imperfect, answers to difficult questions."[1] He goes on to say that the word comes from the same root as eureka. Mathematics is a 'formal heuristic'. Mythos is an 'informal heuristic' and both are tools for making our way in the world. They are merely ways of seeing into and through our experiences.

Interestingly, for a clinician to be glued to a clinical perspective biases the clinician. In this case, what we have is a confirmation bias, also called confirmatory bias or *myside bias*. The myside bias seeks to search for, interpret, favor and recall information in a way that confirms one's preexisting beliefs. A myside bias gives disproportionately less consideration to alternative possibilities. This myside bias is not open-ended. When faced with a challenging situation, as in this account, an embedded confirmation bias limits an

---

[1] Kahneman, Daniel, *Thinking, Fast and Slow*, Farrar, Straus and Giroux, New York, 2011, p. 98. Kahneman received a Nobel Prize in Economics in 2002 for work in decision-making. Amos Tversky, deceased at the time of the award, made a major contribution to this work.

alternative solution. Heuristically, it's like saying, "It's my way or the highway," and winding up in a cul-de-sac.

I don't mean to be hard on the psychiatrist or any clinician who takes on a more objective perspective. But one should be careful to avoid a blindsided outlook.

The psychiatrist did invite the chaplain to the psychiatric ward. What the clinician experienced may have been an imaginative shock.[2] The reaction to the chaplain could have been an expression of bewilderment. One might imagine the clinician saying, "This is not how we deal with patients. What's going on? I've not seen anything as bizarre as this in a medical setting." The psychiatrist has made a move from an objective perspective to an inner one. Here is the possibility for personal transformation—moving from a stance of being a clinician, who tries to maintain distance, to a stance that affirms the subjectivity of the patient. The chaplain affirmed a subjective approach; the patient went willingly into the shower.

Subjectivity and objectivity appear to be two sides of the human psyche or soul. To deny either side is to endanger the whole self. To deny the subjective experience is to kill imagination. When you stop the conversation, you are left with conversation about objective stuff.

Without a 'bridge' or an imaginary link, as well as a felt connection to others, one may experience a very dry place where meaning is slipping away. Living in wonder allows for keeping the conversation open and alive. This is what people do in the social construction of meaning---which could be called 'soul-making.' This human connection is heuristic and suggests Incarnation: "Captain to the bridge!"

"Bridge to the Captain!"

---

[2] Holmes III, Urban T., *Ministry and Imagination,* The Seabury 1981, New York, p. 99. "The 'imaginative shock' is what gets the hermeneutical spiral going." Example: Paul's experience on the road to Damascus was a shock that brought him into a deeper sense of meaning.

L EARNING IS RECIPROCAL!

M any years ago, on a gleaming autumn day, I was stopped by Rahim while walking out of the Turney Center Prison barber shop. Rahim is a bright young inmate who, at the time, wanted to discuss philosophy. He had been reading the dialogues of Plato and aspired to more fully understand Plato's mysterious character, Socrates.

"What do you want to know about Socrates?" I asked.

Rahim replied, "Socrates claimed to know nothing. How can a man who professes ignorance become a legend?"

"What do you know for certain?"

"I know that one and one is two and that night follows day."

"Maybe Socrates, like Jesus, was some sort of ultimate mystery?"

Rahim appeared thoughtful for a few seconds, then continued, "I'm interested in the mysteries. Why don't we get together and discuss Plato? You need to work with us, Chaplain! There's a lot of us who would like to get our teeth into some real meat."

I could hardly believe what I was hearing. My mind drifted back to the time when I took a course in Plato at the University of Florida. As I recalled, the dialogues of Plato seemed very symbolic and imaginative. The scholars had a hard time agreeing on their interpretation of his thought. The professor was so bored with his area of study that he started a nursery and came to class in his dirty work clothes. He never lectured and the class discussion wandered all over the place. Since we live in a pragmatic world, I couldn't imagine a prison philosophy class being able to survive with an outcome of more questions than answers.

I told Rahim, "I don't think the material---a reading on Plato--- will hold their interest."

"That's the problem with you guys," he retorted. "You're not even willing to try anything new."

"All right, big guy," I said. "You get your buddies and come over to the chapel next Saturday night. We'll meet in my office and start reading about the death of Socrates."

To my utter amazement, the group grew to about fifteen. We spent several months reading and discussing excerpts from Plato's *Republic* as well as from a few of his dialogues: *Phaedo, Phaedrus,* and the *Symposium. We* read and discussed thinkers like Carl Jung, James Hillman, Sigmund Freud and Carol Pearson. From our reading of Joseph Campbell, we learned about the twelve stages in the hero's journey.

Later, these men began to pick out topics of personal interest and deliver papers on them. Some of these men wrote stories that spoke to their own experience. There was a great deal of spontaneity in the class---so much that we had to use a monitor to help focus and direct the conversation. What amazed me was that I didn't have to breathe life into the group; it seemed to be incredibly self-organizing. In the process, there appeared to be a transformation taking place in the lives of many who attended the group, including myself, as if it were a kind of distillation. This process generated interest outside the class.

While the group read from the *Phaedrus*, one of the greatest love poems ever written, Phillip told the group that a former teacher said that he was a 'hopeless romantic.' The group listened to his romantic dream of joining with a soul-mate. We witnessed his elation when his long-lost love contacted him; we celebrated with him when he gave an account of his marriage. We helped to hold him together when his beloved started living with another man. With the bursting of Phillip's romantic bubble, he ordinarily would have become extremely violent. That was his past. Having identified with the *Phaedrus*, Phillip knew about the battle with his unruly steed and the great crash, landing him in a place of incarceration.

Phillip read the romantic legend of *Tristan and Iseult* and told us the story from beginning to end. He explored the myth of *Cupid and Psyche* and read the story of *Briar Rose*. In his description of the Briar Rose story, he could imagine the thorn hedge that surrounded this sleeping beauty. He knew that a premature attempt to break thorough an impenetrable hedge would cause him great harm---even more time in prison. After reading Somerset Maugham's *Of Human Bondage*, Phillip saw the problem of compulsive and fixated love. We discussed the character of Ed Leedskalnin, who built the magnificent Coral Castle in Homestead, Florida. He built this engineering masterpiece for a 'sweet sixteen' who failed to return his love. It was a delightful experience to explore with Phillip imaginative ways of remaining a hopeless romantic and living to tell about it. Since leaving Turney Center, I have heard that Phillip has begun a romance with Christianity and may be moving in the direction of a new kind of love---agape.

As the group continued to read the dialogues of Plato, we invariably ran into ways of thinking that seemed absurd with respect to a more contemporary way of thinking. For example, Socrates talked about listening to his daimon or inner voice. In the *Symposium* a character talked about humans being created as hermaphrodites and later splitting apart into both male and female characters. The group got a 'hoot' out of that one. Plato talked about the circulation of the soul throughout the universe. There were invisible powers all around. It appeared to most of the men that this way of thinking just wasn't in touch with the 'real world' or rational living. The problem, of course, was how to make sense of any of this in such a way that it might apply in positive ways to each of our lives.

An approach to this problem came from one of our group members, Gary, who had served as a chaplain in the Air Force. I know of his military background because I was with him when he delivered his military records to the parole board. He had attained the rank of a major and is referred to as 'the Major.' The Major, who has a working knowledge of several languages, kept posting Greek words on the office walls. Gary is very articulate and well read, so much so, that his discourse often few past most of us. It was frustrating, but the group had patience.

At one point, a group member named Mike jokingly called the Major a 'closet fundamentalist'. The Major was furious, left the group for a couple of weeks, but laughed and came back. I guess he came back with a boon because he taught us something about the Socratic Method as well as perspectives from Plato's dialogues.

The crux of what the Major said is this: "We've got to think holistically. Socrates was not just a philosopher; he was a poet. During his life, Socrates used poetic images. He used these images to keep us questioning. Even those things that we take for granted, he questioned. If we have differences, we can reach consensus---like in democracy! The important thing is to keep the dialogue open---like Socrates did!"

From then on, the Major kept referring to this ongoing and questioning dialogue as being peripatetic. Throughout the group activity, he kept reminding us that we were an academy. In mulling over what the Major said, it occurred to me that 'being stuck' in one's personal problems might be, in part, the result of not questioning some fundamental ways of thinking or behaving. The downside of not questioning could be that one is unable to get to the root of a problem and, therefore, make a change. It seems that poetry has a way of opening the imagination and, therefore, enabling people to better direct their lives. Socrates was charged with corrupting the youth of Athens. The questioning and unfolding of new knowledge can lead to change, which can threaten those who have their own interest to protect. The Athenian court crushed the questioning attitude of Socrates and sentenced him to death.

As the group began to read the *Phaedrus,* we learned about Plato's concept of the soul. I began to see our various members in a more poetic light. These men who came to discuss soul were building soul, engaged in an ascent. As in the *Phaedrus*, we are all mounted in individual chariots with our snorting winged horses. Soaring like Zeus and his company, we are each similar to that holographic image yet to come into clear focus. The group itself, with its focus on learning is, at times, a clear image of some well-coordinated fragile whole. Like Plato's charioteers, we are each in the presence of a patron god or (beloved) who characterizes our individual ascent. We all have a white steed and a dark and broken one in the container of our souls, and we dimly see into each other's soul as well as our own.

The strongest part of this image of ascent is something other than pure sexual energy. This image or archetype to which I am referring is what Plato calls Eros. It is the driving force of the soul. Unlike sexual energy, its goal is not tension release. Eros is passion, desire, increased stimulation---it is not so much a push from behind as a pull from the future. In Plato's *Symposium* the character Diotima explains Eros, as a middle region---a metaxy. It is a principle of relatedness between heaven and earth. As in the *Phaedrus*, members of the group are both pushed and pulled toward their heart's desire. Their heart's desire resembles a living presence. It is like an "echo rebounding off rocks." There is the desire to fill an insatiable appetite. But there is absence and, therefore, longing and pain. The dark steed finds passion hard to understand. Freedom entails patience and self-control. Happiness depends on these qualities; the charioteer of our soul is aware of a prison under the earth where fallen souls abide.

This heterogeneous group of inmates reveals itself uniquely in its parts. Gray Wolf affirms Native American traditions, especially in his desire to live in peace and harmony with nature and his brothers. Graywolf had been shipped to a work release center before being released on parole. On what he describes as a beautiful sunny day in downtown Nashville, he and a companion, Fire Heart, suddenly and impulsively left town for a midwestern Native American reservation. This constituted an escape. The reservation where they were headed is a physical place in time and space with an outer well-defined boundary. Gray Wolf states that it would have been a sanctuary had the two of them made it there. However, they were captured and sent back to prison before reaching their destination. As in the Phaedrus, Gray Wolf took a fall landing him back in a place of incarceration.

Mike---I call him by his last name---Stanfield, has his own patron god and his image of the soul points in an unusual direction. In Stanfield's ascent he appears to be committed to absurdity. I don't say this to put Stanfield down, but to lift him up. I say this because the absurdity to which Stanfield is committed does not appear to be connected with drugs, sex and violence---the kind of absurdity he might have been connected with on the street.

Stanfield is a young man serving life plus thirty who walks into my office with the novel entitled *The Stranger* by Albert Camus. He tells me that he has read this book six times, then reads passages aloud to me. I asked Stanfield if he identifies with the main character in the book. His countenance brightens as he says, "Yes, that's me!" As a young existentialist, he experiences the "unreasonable silence of the universe." He knows the experience of the dark horse with broken wings and wakes up in a Kafkaesque underground prison of the absurd. Even in this absurdity, Stanfield is pulled by Eros. Stanfield reads from the final pages of *The Stranger* and is pulled into a kind of commitment to the absurd. He has discovered Sisyphus, whom the gods have condemned to ceaselessly roll a rock to the top of a mountain, a rock that will continually roll down again after reaching the top. As in Plato's *Phaedrus*, Stanfield is finding moisture and beginning to sprout wings in that "place of incarceration." His beloved is in the imaginal possibilities that lie ahead. The form it takes is in creative writing. He is discovering a centerless center in a literal prison with a real spatial center.

S.R. Hudson is Stanfield's close friend. He is also a young writer and has brought one of his stories to the group. Hudson writes about the wounds that shame leaves behind. He knows how to grieve over the dark horse of stubbornness and ignorance. He also can grieve over the shaming charioteer and white steed whose connectedness he desires. His unique contribution to the divine is that, without deep grief over parts of our own soul or the souls of others, we can never be trusted and included in the celestial flight. Hudson's young wings are moist from his fierce tears.

Gary, the Major I mentioned earlier, is well aware of the circular motion or the eternal return of the soul's journey. His telos is to return home with a boon. He wants to expose the archetypal images of narrowness, conspiracy, and violence. He wants to expose the violent retributive human forms of these images. Gary's beloved or patron god appears to be the Warrior deity. This deity does not appear to be one of violence, but one who fights to stay in the battle when the battle for truth heats up. This god is his patron of staying power. Gary brings the gift of staying power and soars high in flight. I think that he has reached Plato's 'vault of heaven,' but I am not sure that he has yet been set in orbit around the heavens---an orbit that carries winged souls to a view of the "heaven beyond the heavens." It will be interesting to see how, or even whether, Gary comes back down to earth to stall and nourish his steeds.

Joe, another interesting character who comes to the group, tells us that he is a pagan and prefers polytheism to monotheism. I believe that Joe is right when he claims that his patron god is Hermes. The term hermetic is derived from the pagan god, Hermes. He is a deity with wings on his heels that enable him to be a carrier of souls and messages, something like a trickster or a rogue. Like Hermes, Joe carries me, and probably others in the group, across boundaries of the soul. Along the way, one is apt to be both stimulated with

109

his insight and horrified at the same time. Joe's intellectual stimulation is felt and acknowledged when he delivers a paper on hallucinogenic substances and experiences that alter consciousness.

In discussing the behavior of Gyges in Plato's *Republic*, Joe explains the horizontal oscillation of soul, creating a play of opposites. His example is the tension that exists between the individual and society when society does not affirm individual rights or protect them. To avoid being stuck in duality, Joe says, "Just because Gyges became invisible, killed the king, and took his wife, doesn't make him a bad person---truth is relative."

Shock or horror also comes when Joe talks about 'annihilating' some unjust soul. At this point, the hermetic Joe is set in place; chariots lose wheels, horses lower their heads, and raise their tails against the earth's gravitational field. When the counterbalancing mechanism of duality comes apart, chariots collide, wings are crushed, and souls are trampled and broken in an agonizing descent. Joe, as guide of souls, has brought us to the illumination of the underworld. The telos of Joe's hermetic soul is protean; it changes form and roams all over the place. His messages bring experiences of surprise, ranging from the heights of joy to the depths of sorrow. Joe may not grow wings, but he has them on his heels. Now that Joe has been paroled, it will be interesting to see if this type of hermetic imagining takes him back to prison.

I had to ask myself what it was that was so magical about this small group. Those who showed up were certainly open to expressing themselves. I think that they all believed in a higher power. Many of the men said that they would not come to a traditional religious service because they felt that they would be indoctrinated. They resisted hypocrisy and mental manipulation.

Learning to live is what these men were contemplating in these informal studies. By writing papers and sharing their own stories, they built self-esteem and respect for others. Through poetic images, as in the *Phaedrus*, these men saw into and through the problems of handling emotions and anger.

Most inmates I encounter are struggling with their souls. They reach out beyond themselves. Fundamentally, they want to know where they come from, how to live, and where their fate or destiny is taking them. They seem to be in search of a meaningful life, whatever that may be. This is what the philosophy class at Turney Center was all about. All of the members of the group, including myself, reflected on our frustrations, compulsions, and fixations. However, when an inmate came into the group who had a fixed agenda and attempted to exercise 'mind-control' or establish himself as some sort of guru, he didn't last---his appearance vanished, and no one told him to disappear.

Keeping the conversation open, being in touch with others, relates to a spiritual journey. There is something self-organizing about an ongoing dialogue, where folks have staying power. They take the knocks and keep coming back. This can take place, I think, in most groups, whether it be a philosophy class, an AA group, or a Sunday school class.

Over time, something like fermentation brings fresh results, which can't be forced into being. Lives are changed, and most of the time, the process is gradual. Fixations, compulsions and rage can diminish or be channeled into positive creative expression.

As time passes, we become more aware of who we are and where we're destined, but we are never finished products---not completely. In the end, what we have to offer is never a 'quick fix' to be handed out like an over-the-counter elixir. What we share with others is the pain and joy of our experiences along the way. We can link with others, but we can never live their lives for them. Every person, at some point, must bear the responsibility for his life choices and discover what it means to live with others. In so doing, he can discover what it means to live. Learning is reciprocal.

HEROIC JUSTIFICATION

By S. R. Hudson

The right front tire was flat, but I was driving slowly so it wasn't hard to steer. The year was 1977 and the car was a ten-year-old Bonneville. Cheap Trick was playing "I Want You to Want Me" on the radio, and my brother Shane was trying to sing along. We were stoned. It was a perfect July afternoon, and everything was right with the world. I just wish we knew it then...

I pulled over to the curb and my brother laboriously stuttered, "H-h-hey, m-man, there's a p-pay phone o-o-over there b-b-by the p-park m-m-man!"

"Hey, right on!" I said. "Here's a dime man. Why don't cha call the Mod Squad or somthin'...and while you're at it tell'em to bring a jack and a spare, okay?"

Then he said something stupid. "Aw, aw, aw, aw, okay, okay. I, I, I see, I see man." Then he turned and walked towards the phone.

Some girls in a yellow convertible VW bug screeched to a stop almost hitting him. The driver, an obnoxious blond, yelled, "Why don't cha watch where you're walking, freak-boy!"

Shane's face turned blood red and I thought he might do something crazy, but all he said was, "I, I, I'm s-s-s-sorry."

113

Both girls laughed at him and drove away. He dropped his head and continued his trek towards the phone. I turned my attention toward the flat tire. If he looked over at me, I didn't want him to think I had noticed what had happened. Some young boys from the local Pee-Wee league were practicing with their coach. The little boy who was at bat kept jumping backwards every time the ball was pitched his way. All the other boys were laughing at him, and his coach seemed to be furious. He placed four or five bats on the ground behind the boy and said, "If you jump back again, you will trip and fall---so keep your damn eyes on the damn ball and concentrate! Now, let's play ball!"

As the pitcher got ready to throw a sweet curve-ball, I noticed Shane had dropped the phone receiver he'd been speaking into. He had both his hands placed flatly against the glass window of the phone booth; he was staring intently at the scene unfolding before him. The little white ball spun towards the batter in a silent lazy arch. I could see the terror in his young eyes; it was a familiar expression. Then the youngster closed his eyes and jumped backwards again. It was an amazing jump. He cleared all the bats. The other boys broke out in hysterics. The coach was not laughing. His eyes were open wide, and his nostrils were flaring. He put me in mind of the Conan character from the comic books. He walked over to the boy and pushed him to the ground. Pointing his finger in the kid's face, he screamed. "You dumb little bastard, what are you some kind of patsy queer?"

As the coach raged on, I heard a loud thumping; it was Shane in the phone booth smashing his fist against the glass. Then he sprung the door and ran faster than I ever saw him run in his life. He snatched up a bat that happened to be leaning against the fence without breaking stride. It happened so fast the irate coach never even knew what hit him. Yet, I saw it all in separate steady frames as if the whole scene had been laid out in a series of thirty-five-millimeter picture stills. The wooden Louisville-Slugger connected with the back of the coach's head flipping his cap into the air. The blow sounded like a great slab of beef smacking the tile floor of a butcher shop. As the coach dropped, a westward breeze sent the cap drifting into left field. The poor pitiful man was probably dead from the first whack, but Shane didn't stop there. Rapidly and with expert concentration, he continued to bash the fellow's skull until it was the consistency of jello. I couldn't move. My black engineer's boots seemed to be cemented to the tarmac. Then it was over. Shane stood straight and turned to the kid who hadn't budged an inch while his teammates had run screaming in terror from the park. In the gentlest voice I ever heard and without stuttering a bit, my brother said, "Never be afraid to be afraid." The boy didn't react at all. He just stood there, motionless and silent, with a dull and distant gaze.

As Shane walked back to the car, I got a feeling in my gut. It was too much. I recalled the putrid flavor of rotted apples and I fell to my knees, heaving pinkish orange chunks of my half-digested lunch. The sight of this in combination with the heavy acidic aftertaste of vomit brought on another round of gut-wrenching tremors. Shane knelt low behind me and placed his hand on my shoulder. Patting me softly, he uttered a genuinely surrealistic prayer.

"Oh Lord," he began. "Forgive these arrogant fools; they know not who they cross, nor what cross the crossed bare in their wake; for compassion is at stake, vengeance is wine, and the wine is fine, savored with pity and tempered with justice---a lesson for posterity, Amen."

With this, he stood up and walked to the car. "You comin', m-m-man?"

His stutter had returned. We drove away on a flat and somehow made it to the river. I hated to lose that car. It held a lot of great memories for me. But machines are replaceable. My brother, the stuttering insane champion of meek, traumatized, and victimized Little League baseball players, was not. That afternoon in July of '77 marked a turning point in our relationship. I gained a crude kind of respect for Shane that day---not as you may erroneously deduce, for he had murdered a man in cold blood. Rather, because, for a brief moment, he had stood up for himself and every other kid who had ever been pushed around, abused, bullied and mistreated by the mindless and arrogant fools of the world. We each choose our own heroes for our own reasons it seems. My own brother may be mine.

Commentary

By J.H. Welborn

The author, S. R. Hudson, states elsewhere, "I have looked into the mirror of my soul and there I have seen shame! Shame that withers a man in his youth, steals away his pride. Ravaged by attrition, it curbs ambition, leaving little will to live---a desperate compromise!"

Where is our shame? Is it in our wounds? What do we do with that three-legged Volkswagen after it has "stood up for itself" and been "tempered by justice?" We hate to lose our transportation; it holds "lots of great memories." When the vehicle is buried in the river of the subconscious will it rise again? How will it move through the landscape on a flat tire? How will it stand up for justice?

Robert Bly, in *Iron John*, a book about men, says, "Those with no wounds are the unluckiest of all. (Of course, one can't think that, because no such person has ever been found.) Men are taught over and over when they are boys that a wound that hurts is shameful. A wound that stops you from continuing to play is a girlish wound. He who is truly a man keeps walking, dragging his guts behind."[1]

In *II Samuel*, Absalom, the son of David, failed to have a personal encounter with his own woundedness. Absalom murdered his brother Ammon for the rape of Tamar their sister. In time, David received his Absalom from exile. "In all of Israel there was not a man so highly praised for his handsome appearance as Absalom. From the top of his head to the sole of his foot there was no blemish in him" (II Sam

---

[1] Robert Bly, *Iron John*, Addison-Wesley Publishing Company, Inc., New York, 1990, pp. 41-42.

14:25). In the end, Absalom went against his father's army and was killed.

Robert Bly goes on to say, "That where a man's wound is, that is where his genius will be. Wherever the wound appears in our psyches, whether from alcoholic father, shaming mother, shaming father, abusing mother, whether it stems from isolation, disability, or disease, that is precisely the place for which we will give our major gift to the community."[2]

How will the sons face their wounds if the fathers do not teach them how to properly carry them? The initiation into manhood requires the father. It takes the elders to model and teach the transformation of woundedness. The fathers do not shoot their wounded sons; they help them discover and develop a hidden treasure.

04/04/1997

---

[2] Ibid. p. 42.

THE LAXATIVE

By Mike Stanfield

It was because of the laxative that Michael Steinman, in his mere eighth year of life, suffered as he never suffered before.

His mother, undoubtedly well-intentioned, had given him the surprisingly small pill with his oatmeal, after he had somehow mentioned, in casual conversation, his run-in with minor constipation. You see, he had not yet learned to keep certain things to himself---such as a slightly hardened stool---and his complaint had provoked in his mother a reflex not unlike that which causes, say, momma birds to feed and groom baby birds.

"Take this and you'll feel better," she had said, probably assuming he would have ample opportunity to achieve regularity at school. She must have pictured an unrestrained world of clean, well-stocked bathrooms, which Michael could freely choose to visit at any time he wished, like some God-given right promised in that Pledge of Allegiance his school masters insisted he repeat each morning. Little did she know of the strict world her son existed in each day, a world absent of liberty, free speech, and where in-class restroom requests were suspect and granted only as rare, undeserved gifts.

He had been in the BOY'S ROOM, after the morning recess. A small eternity ago. It was nothing less than custom to stop and loiter there before waiting in line at the water fountain, a futile attempt at making recreation time last longer. He remembered with longing that crowded and chaotic place of talking and laughing and pissing in the long and aging porcelain urinal. One boy had made the forbidden "frog's eye" in one of the sinks by covering the drain with a brown paper towel; he poked it when it bubbled. But the idea of performing serious business there did not materialize, and Michael had forgotten entirely that little pill.

Of course, if the Urge <u>had</u> set upon him, at that moment he would have been unable to accommodate it, with every boy in the Second Grade his immediate and unavoidable audience. The stalls sometimes had no toilet paper; a few of them were missing their seats (those large, forked and industrial toilet seats---like you find at any public place or institution---were less than adequate, anyway). <u>Not</u> <u>one</u> of them had a door. It was as if the school bigwigs---the Principal, the Principal's Secretary, the hairless Janitor, who was always spreading that stinking floor buff powder all around---left the stall doors off intentionally in an unreasonable plot to discourage in-school defecation. You were forced to sit unshielded, a stranded spectacle for any and everyone who entered the lavatory. Even during class-time it was unsafe; there was always a straggler, another nomad-restroom-user like yourself, intruding and carrying in his back pocket the obligatory, usually oversized and wooden hall pass like a gas station restroom key.

But the single witness to your act was nothing compared to a mass audience. There you'd be: sitting and minding your own, in performance of the most natural act, and presto, an entire class---maybe Ms. Johnson's first-grade or worse, Mrs. Maylor's fourth---appears from the playground, first one boy, maybe two. They don't say anything, for a second. Then five more come; now seven, fifteen. The room fills with laughing, hideous creatures, who gather at the gaping doorway of your stall in tight, changing clusters, like sadistic, heckling bees, until every boy has taken his long turn laughing and screaming and pointing at the poor slob taking a dump at the wrong time. Surely, there were few things worse than that.

Of course, Michael realized, and not without increased yearning, he could have pulled the old wait-around-until-everyone's-gone trick, if the urge had come. But it hadn't, so he didn't. And much time had passed since then. A lunch of chili dogs and chocolate milk had come and gone; and he, as you might say to a grownup, had "to go," like never before. The possible presence of a bathroom witness could not discourage him now.

It didn't seem possible to sweat at the same time one is cold, but it was happening, nonetheless. The pain in his abdomen, perhaps not unlike a cowboy's gunshot wound, had spread its way, snakelike, through different areas of his guts until he felt its bold attempt at escape. It was its relentless effort to get out which now caused the most pain and concern. Michael wondered if they would ever stop reading.

He had known better than to ask Ms. Spinch if he could go to the BOYS' ROOM during the reading period. Ms. Spinch was a Second-Grade teacher perhaps hardened by job dissatisfaction and age. She was a gangly figure with a head of steadfast, white curls, with hidden eyes in the back of her head. She had no patience for children and made no secret of it. She was generally beastly to all of them, but for Michael she seemed to reserve a singular intolerance. She often assailed him for his chronic inattention or his illegible handwriting or his lateness to school. He was quite terrified of the old woman and her many large and gaudy necklaces, her loud and nearly offensive perfume (which was somehow intimidating by itself), and her pinch. He had witnessed many times her habit of towing someone around by his (or her) ear or cheek to combat daydreaming or impertinence. It had happened to him. She also liked to pinch your checks together, using her thumb and index finger like the claws of a colossal crab, and then, with your mouth shaped into a deformed, involuntary "O," she shook your head back and forth. "Do you hear me," she might say, shaking you by the skin of your face, "Do you hear me?" And all the while, you are immersed in that suffocating, malodorous stench, a sickening semi-sweetness, which lingers long after she is gone.

It was from such methods of torture---her ear/cheek/face-pinching---that Ms. Spinch came to be known as Ms. "Pinch," but, of course, only behind her back and, secretly, in the thoughts of those she plagued. And around her sympathizers.

As the reading continued, Michael sustained a dread of being called upon. It would of course begin with Ms. Spinch humiliating him for not keeping up, as he knew not the chapter nor the page. Even worse, he would have to read---that is, read without allowing his voice to betray his straining efforts at controlling his bowels. A vision of a conflict with his teacher made him shudder. He knew he could endure an episode of tug-of-ear.

Presently, the current reader was stopped, and he waited in the resulting hush with much trepidation for the announcement of the next one. He could feel the hunger in Ms. Spinch's probe, as she surely scanned the class for her next victim. He dared not look at her now, lest their eyes meet and expose his damnable inattention, the curse of the Medusa. Michael was reminded of that woman in the Bible who wasn't supposed to look back: behold Ms. Spinch, and you'll turn into a pillar of salt!

At last she called on Suzy Robinson, who sat just ahead of Michael; and he---relieved, but only fleetingly---watched his desktop, pretending to read along with her colorless voice, which, like the other before her, exhibited none of the cadences and accents of conversational speech but, instead, droned into Michael's ears like a punishment. Bang! Pow! Crash! her words said to him, each one as meaningless and as unintelligible as the next; each one a physical blow, accenting by degrees the pain he was experiencing. His face felt flushed from its toleration. It would be quite unfortunate, he mused, to give in to his torment, after coming so far and enduring so long. Pooping in his pants would be a grand tragedy indeed.

They called it Number 2. It didn't make sense, really---not in light of its significance over urination, which they called Number 1. Michael incessantly confused the colloquialisms whenever confronted with them. "Is it Number 1 or Number 2," someone would ask, to which he invariably said the opposite of what he intended to perform. Perhaps peeing was designated Number 1 due to its frequency, but that wasn't a very good reason; its quantity negating the other's quality. At least at this moment, it was Number 2 which was number one on Michael's mind.

Except for the omnipresent hums of the air conditioning and florescent lighting, the room again went quiet. The reading had ended. Ms. Spinch chalked "PAGE 87" on the board and said, "You know what to do. Answer the questions; this is not a talking time." The room filled with the noises of notepads slapping desks, of students shuffling and sighing in the pursuit of their labors, of the frictional, abrasive growl of the pencil sharpener. At last Michael's moment of salvation had arrived, and he quit his desk in which he had endured so much torture. He could almost hear the joyous string music at the end of <u>THE LION KING</u> or an episode of <u>Lassie</u>, another happy ending you knew (though, perhaps, subconsciously) would come, but just didn't know how. He would prevail after all, he realized, and the thought of sitting on one of those bulky toilet seats, the exuberant relief and quenching of his urgent, particular desire, actually loosened his bowels further. It was only the encouragement of impeding relief which now gave him the strength to persevere and suppress The Urge more intensely.

"Ms. Spinch," he said before he reached her desk, careful to employ the second <u>S</u>, "may I have the hall pass, I-----."

Simply, she said, "No."

He watched her expression a moment before understanding the meaning of her word, its resoluteness.

"Return to your seat," she said, staring hard through the bifocals fixed to her nose. "You're not going to get away with your laziness this time, Mr. Steinman. Sit down and finish your assignment."

"But--"

"Sit." It was hopeless, and he felt the vehemence in every step he took toward his desk. Faces he passed, cruel and distorted, looked up at him with indifference to his agony; they had no empathy to spare, and on he forged. Alone in his suffering.

The assignment. If he could only answer the questions at the end of the story. Michael felt the hot madness of hope well-up inside of him, and he despaired. To hope is to rise above apathy, but the better of the two conditions is relative to one's immediate position. In apathy, struggle disappears, and there is at last rest and reprieve from worry, fear and effort, the sweet sleep of death. He had embraced without question that the request could be refused. Did she, he wondered, actually believe he was lying? Alas, he knew it did not matter. The results were the same. There was only one question facing him now: Could he make it? His devotion to hope was proving a burdensome addiction.

He remembered the severity of his pain when he sat down, as he fairly reeled through several exquisite shudders inside him. If he had known the names and the specifics of his internal devices, he would have realized that the excruciating pain in his gut was caused by a hefty measure of fecal material expanding and pushing against the soft, bulging walls of his rectal cavity. His intestines pushed inward like shit-filled sausages, squeezing and forcing their contents into the anal canal, the final passage, the point of no return. Michael Steinman's only relief would come from full defecation, and the involuntary muscles system of his lower digestive tract would not rest until that occurred. All of them---the muscles of his ascending, transverse and descending colon, the muscles of his pelvic floor and rectum---all pushed and increased pressure against his final bastion of defense: the internal and external sphincters, the only voluntary muscles of the lot. All hope depended on the success of these small, ring-like tissues.

124

The Laxative

Like a man who still shoots his six-gun despite the arrows in his back, Michael Steinman found his pencil and carefully, taking measured breaths, scratched his name in the proper place on his paper. Page 87 had six true or false questions, and he numbered his paper from one to six before the pain inside him stopped his pencil. It was an incredibly acute agony, which focused most intently at one place in particular, the point of ejection. His sphincters, performing as a palsied floodgate, cried out to him, exhausted.

Tightly, Michael closed his eyes; it was just a wave, like the others, which would diminish in intensity after a moment. He was closer than ever; all he had to do was open his eyes and write "true" and "false" several times, if the pain would just--

Bright light blinded him in the darkness behind his eyelids, a brightness accompanied at once by a new, exquisite, fleeting pain: it hurt so much he could no longer detect it---anti-pain. He cringed because he knew it was supposed to hurt: his anguish had become a habit. But it hurt no more. He felt a wet warmth spreading in his pants and realized with relief and horror it was over.

Nearby, dryly, someone coughed.

He was sitting on a horrible thing; he was saddened with the heaviness of warm quicksand. It was, fortunately, not liquefied enough to escape down the shoot of his pant-leg, but it, nevertheless, filled the crevice of his buttocks and spread substantially over his butt cheeks. The wet, velvety, lard-like mass reminded him of a thick and impossibly warm milkshake.

He stole glances at others around him. They didn't seem to realize his deed. Michael took a speculative but furtive survey of the air and detected no corruption. He dared to think of what would happen if they discovered his secret, and the curse of hope intervened once more. Maybe they would not find out; maybe he could make it until he was home. Safe. Two hours. He concentrated on writing "true" and "false" in a varying order, sickened by the mushiness in his pants.

125

When his paper bore six answers, Michael Steinman placed his pencil in the groove at the top of his desk and waited. He appraised the work of his neighbors. Terry Rayner had five questions answered and sucked on her eraser in genuine concentration before writing the final "false" there. Clay Hedgeman's paper lay completed under his elbows. He crossed his eyes and stuck out his tongue, ending Michael's survey and sparking someone's inane laugh.

"Place your papers on my desk when you're finished," Ms. Spinch said mechanically, initiating a mass migration toward the front of the room. The problem of walking hadn't occurred to Michael, and with futility he asked those passing his desk to carry his paper with theirs. The first two ignored him, while fat Stephanie simply laughed. She, of red hair and redder checks, always seemed under the impression he was playing some fool prank or other nonsense and laughed whenever he spoke to her. His only option was to take it himself. He cheered himself with the idea the walk would be practice for later, when he had to go outside for recess and, after that, all the way to the school bus.

If he had known the scientific composition of the mire in his pants, he would have realized most of it was water and indigestible food matter (which was mainly bacterial debris, with some degree of fats, proteins and cellulose). But he was as unaware of the chemical makeup of fecal material as he was of the fact that the laxative, as is its nature, had caused his intestines to empty completely, instead of merely partly, as is with average bowel movements. The resulting mass, probably nearing an entire pound of excrement, weighed on him heavily as he left his desk. He took an experimental step forward and cringed at the viscous flux he felt down there. He considered the possibility of making it all the way home in such a condition. Perhaps it could be done. Why, all he had to do was walk (he took two more casual steps) and pretended he was normal, that he was one of THEM, that he --

"He peed in his pants," the hysterical voice of Glenn Sicery screamed to the world. "Michael Steinman peed in his pants!"

The classroom became animated with spontaneous giggling, and Michael, frozen in time, heard fat Stephanie say, undoubtedly with a hand cupped to her gaping mouth, "Ummmm...!" "You peed in your pants," Glen Sicery said, reveling in his discovery. Pointing, he laughed: "He, he, heee!"

"It's not pee," said Michael.

The class seemed to lurch backward an instant before it comprehended. But, save for fat Stephanie's intensified "Ummm...", the incredulity did not last. The laughter, this time severe and hearty, bellowed from everyone Michael saw. Glenn Sicery, delighted beyond belief, buckled toward the floor in mirthful convulsions. The classroom had turned into a menagerie of pointing fingers, tear-stained eyes and wild, laughing faces, many going scarlet from want of oxygen. It was something like the sea-sick, spinning cinematography of some 50's movie depicting insanity. Faces and voices swirled and mixed, faded and reappeared; around, around, around they encircled him, their guffaws prodding and poking and poking him like ... like ... like nothing at all.

It didn't hurt.

All the laughter, despite the dreadfulness of its origin was not, it occurred to him, the terrible monster he had dreaded so profoundly. He had mentally cringed at the onslaught of attention and expected degradation of being a laughing stock. But it didn't hurt; it was not the agony he expected---no, it was something else, something almost pleasant.

The laughter was contagious.

Though he had the vague idea he should scream or cry or run away, his only feeling was joy---joy at the termination of his suffering, joy at the mirth he had caused: it was over, and people were laughing. It was like some backward world, where pain brings pleasure and defeat begets some secret, personal form of victory. His shame had evaporated with the cold sweat on his face.

Not unaware of his own smile, he played the scene by walking slow and stiff-legged, his arms out-stretched, like

127

Frankenstein's monster with doo-doo in his drawers, and the laughter reached an uproarious peak. Something grabbed him and pulled him away. He looked and saw the angry face of Ms. Spinch, who was leading him out of the classroom and down the hallway. "You think it's funny, don't you?" she said, strangely out of breath. "Trying to get back at me!" She led him by the arm in her usual, tyrannical manner. For once, however, she left alone his ears and cheeks.

They came to the kindergarten room, and the teacher there, a much younger woman, with motherly warmth in her eyes, listened with warmth to Ms. Spinch's account of the accident, while several kids, out of ear-shot, looked on wide-eyed and curious. "We can fix you right up," she said to Michael and went to a cupboard. She returned with a pair of pants and underwear. "Maybe these will fit," she said.

In ridiculously short (nearly up to his knees) and loudly orange and plaid pants, Michael Steinman walked the blacktop perimeter in thought. He pretended, as he sometimes did during recess, to be in a race car, making loops around a track, but mainly he pondered his discovery. It was quite a relief to be free of his burden. Upon his return to the classroom, after donning the fresh and odd clothes, the laughter had died and only Glen Sicery's burgeoning, gap-toothed grin indicated anything had happened. At once Michael missed the spotlight. The attention of the entire class had been upon him, and he had made them laugh. The fact that he had defecated on himself no longer carried much significance. After all, it had worked out, in the end.

Recess concluded, and he, walking slowly back inside, alone, wondered what his next act of buffoonery would be--- something deliberate, this time, but just as effective as shitting on oneself, but without the mess. He had the vague idea he was treading the unexplored territory of destiny, the possible discovery of his life's calling. Like flowers growing atop cow dung, there was somewhere in the perpetration or experience of his nasty accident, a prize to be discovered. In excreting that seemingly inopportune load of fecal matter, Michael sensed a clue or hint to his purpose in the world and deciphering just exactly what that was felt like a challenge. And he felt giddy at its invitation.

In the BOYS' ROOM he found a crowd gathered around the garbage can, enthralled by its contents.

"Oooh, look at it," said a red-headed boy from another class, another grade. "Gross," someone said.

Though Michael knew the object of their fascination, he too peered into the trash can and saw the shit-laden underwear, twisted into a disgusting wad. No one seemed to know where it had come from. "Gross!" exclaimed Michael.

I HAVE AN ANSWER!

By Phillip J. Jordon

My name is Phillip J. Jordon. I am a convict at Turney Center Prison in Only, Tennessee.

It occurred to me that the men and women who were appointed by the mayor of Nashville for the purpose of solving Nashville's murder epidemic are, for the most part, good upstanding and law-abiding citizens. How could they know what causes people turn to crime in the first place? I've been justly locked away for nearly a decade, so I have insight into the psyche of the criminal mind that cannot be gained in college or in any other manner, except by the way I myself have studied this subject---from personal experience.

Over the years that I have been locked away, I have heard, first hand, every conceivable story behind the actions of prisoners. More important, I've delved into the lifestyles that these men led before coming to prison. I, myself, stumbled upon my own rehabilitative beginnings, only by the grace of God. Although religion alone is not the answer, God helps those who help themselves.

The common denominator that links every story of every man is the lack of mentorship and wholesome guidance. Men have an inherent instinct to seek respect and approval from their peers, parents, women, and others. Our fathers and grandfathers, and even men we don't know

131

personally, have homes, cars, and families---signs of respect in everyone's eyes.

Our fathers learned from our grandfathers how to gain these things through teaching good morals, hard work and right from wrong. Generation X, The Pepsi Generation, and Generation Next are not getting this kind of wholesome mentorship that our fathers received, because in this day and age, one income will not provide for a family. Often our parents are forced to work two or more jobs in order to attempt to meet these growing monetary needs for the family. Our parents are unavailable to invest the time necessary for teaching their children these morals.

Our grandparents are having to work longer before reaching retirement age and also are unavailable to our young people, or they are being pushed aside into old folks' homes and rendered useless, which leaves America's young people to seek respect and approval among themselves. They are without the benefit of good moral teachings and mentorship.

For example, more often than not, our young people fail to become successful in life and either turn to drugs to escape from their failures or to become willing to risk selling drugs in order to get ahead to survive comfortably. Our parents and grandparents were able to do this, in the past, by respectable means. Also, among these types of risky means to get ahead are robbery, theft, burglary, bad checks, fraud, etc. The list goes on and on. All of these are bad moral choices; so, you should understand this...making the baby boomer generation work longer is leaving far fewer jobs for our young people to move into. Desperation to achieve comfortable lives becomes hopeless for our young people without those jobs.

Furthermore, our elders <u>are</u> the answer to solving our nation's crime and murder epidemic! They are far from useless after retirement! In fact, they are our greatest asset and are, indeed, America's only hope.

Here is the answer you have been waiting for. First, let's begin with our school-age children before they become criminals. I'm not talking about formal education, but moral

I Have an Answer

mentorship as a mandatory additional class, which can be taught by our, otherwise, useless elderly citizens serving as volunteers. This would give our elderly a new and all-important purpose in life and, at the same time, expose our young children to good wholesome moral values that most of them would not otherwise have the opportunity to learn.

Second, America's young adults who fail and end up before a judge can be sentenced to more than just probation or community service as punishment but, in addition, be required to attend an old folks' home to volunteer an hour or two each week to care for and visit our elderly citizens. This will not only provide exposure for our young adults to good moral teaching from our elderly citizens, but also give this group of elderly citizens a purpose and usefulness. A sense of compassion could develop between people from different generations.

Third and finally, for the men, women, and even juveniles who already have made terrible decisions and wound up in prison, this is called the Department of Correction, but there is no correction involved in this environment. These people (despite the common public belief) search in vain for rehabilitation, to find out where, in their thinking, they went wrong, and more often than not, they are unable to learn anything from their time spent in this environment except how to become better criminals. More than anywhere else, the men, women, and juveniles in prison need a volunteer mentor program. After all, these are going to become your future neighbors. So, it should be important to you to introduce correct thinking and to expose them to the good moral ideas that they seriously had no way of knowing. How can anyone ever be expected to know what they have never been exposed to?

After 29 years of mistakes and screw ups and nine years of punishment, I have sought to become more spiritually in tune with my conscience, something I never knew I had before. Having a conscience helps a person not to place blame on any group of people. After all, each of us is responsible for his own actions. Because it is a well-known fact that there are two baby boomers for every young person in America, we should embrace the older generation as a valuable resource. They are the mentors for our young people and our wayward young adults who are the future of our country.

Think about it, how much worse would this country be in today without the morals and the wisdom of our predecessors? I believe The Big Brother/Big Sister program was a good idea, but it didn't target the right groups of troubled people who needed the mentorship most. I just thought I'd give you some perspective from someone who has been where you may not go, to prison. I've seen and experienced what you can't completely learn from any book. I've experienced mentorship from both staff and older inmates. I sincerely hope that my suggestions have given insight and might help you in your quest to solve Nashville's crime epidemic. This may not be the total solution to all our current problems, but it is a starting point to get back on track.

NATURAL LAW INTO THE MILLENNIUM

By Major Gary W. Phelps

Natural Law is a term which has been assumed to be included in the vocabulary among any sector or individual within the "religious." The most common definition among the citizens of the republic, for "natural law," is that all citizens are endowed with certain God-given inalienable rights, "... life, liberty and the pursuit of happiness ...." In the 1770's, the U.S. Constitution, the old one, acknowledged that the future of the republic hinged upon the consent of the governed to a system of government that did not deny the citizen his inalienable rights.

Natural law included the separation of church and state, which determined that government was ruled by reason, with the only stipulation that the religious, who were citizens, would not be held to obey any law or statute that was contrary to the Word of God such as the Ten Commandments.

This was the genius of the authors manifested in the U.S. Constitution! They were well versed in the historic tragedies where states controlled churches and religions could govern a nation. The past history of holy wars in continental Europe served to demonstrate the purpose of natural law, i.e., separation of church and state in general, and in particular, the right of the individual to choose. Now, the

136

U.S. Constitution which was written by genius in the 1770's is under siege by the buffoons.

Natural law is not to be confused with natural selection of the species nor rassenkunde (German: racial science). Natural law, as defined in the U.S. Constitution would sustain "due process," "equal protection," and "privileges and immunities" of national citizenship. No state can remove those rights from the citizen without due process of law, especially sovereign immunity ("The King can do no wrong!"). This includes both procedural law (i.e., government action), and substantive law (i.e., the content of the law itself). The central feature for the citizen in all matters, even religion, is the right to choose. This includes the right not to choose religion at all.

The genius of the authors of the U.S. Constitution was unilateral and allowed the constituency (that is us, folks! We, the people!) to change with the continual emerging evolution of society in the USA to involve such matters as Bible reading, bus transportation, financial aid, released time, school prayers, standing, and Sunday closing laws.

Freedom of religion into the 1990's deals with conscientious objectors (those who do not inhale), flag salutes and public schools, Sunday closing laws and even unemployment compensation.

The establishment of religion in America and the practice of it has been so academic and broad that acceptance and practice becomes obscure. A lack of commitment leads to complacency, whether the practice is to hatch (baptize), match (marry) or dispatch (bury). This is one end of the spectrum. On the other end of the spectrum, is the gray area in regard to freedom of expression.

Freedom of expression includes a host of scenarios: access to information, access to media, access to private property, and access to public property. There are shades of gray in the advocacy of legal acts such as the balance of the rights of the individual as opposed to the group. This would include commercial speech, demands for information, demonstrations and mass protest. Freedom of expression also deals with hostile audiences, incitement, indecency, libel and subversive advocacy. Those scenarios for freedom of expression are not exhaustive. Each matter is resolved on a case-by-case basis in the endless pursuit of consensus.

The pursuit of consensus was in chaos as it went into the new millennium, as the 1990's has revealed. The tenet of a representative republic (the consent of the citizens to be governed, in tandem with accountability of authority to the constituency) has been the foundation of the U.S. Constitution since the inception of this nation as a republic. Our elected officials and experts in any echelon of the state and the nation, were from diverse backgrounds and occupations (e.g., the farmer, doctor, businessman, et. al.). However, in the 1990's, with rare exception, our elected officials were lawyers, deeming themselves entitled to acquire for themselves the right to choose in all matters, while the citizens are to succumb to their decisions in unquestioning obedience. This is not the republic, but sovereign immunity ("The King can do no wrong!").

The tenet of a representative republic has its own expression in religion concerning any denomination or faith group, regardless of tradition. They selected a leadership that would conduct their affairs with a sense of accountability to the membership, and, in turn, their allegiance to the sacred text or belief standards. The search for excellence was the pursuit of the "brightest and the best" in the constituency regardless of race, creed, color, or social station. However, ecclesiastical elitism has invaded the religious. Over the decades, family oligarchies and self-styled structures of apostolic succession have resulted in religious feudal regimes. Those feudal regimes have evolved to masquerade their own philosophical beliefs as the religious standard for their respective constituencies, even to the extent that the traditional sacred text and/or standards of belief have been set aside.

The key determination is "the right to change," which is the right of the constituency in the sacred and the secular. However, in the 1990's ecclesiastical elitists determined that it is their prerogative to keep for themselves "the right to change," and to force their will on the respective constituencies. This, of course, is masqueraded as in the best interest of the constituency or as a compelling government interest. In both sacred doctrine or secular substantive law and sacred practice or secular procedural law, the result is the same. The constituency is conquered when authority in the sacred or secular no longer has any degree of accountability to the citizen or citizens. The masquerade is a lie which violates the essence of authentic approach to natural law.

In the 1990's, religious denominations and faith groups of any tradition were plagued by what sacred authority considers "defectors." These so-called defectors withdrew to alternative faith/religious communities. They had no representation in leadership. The sham excuse of ecclesiastical elitists was that defectors had lost allegiance. In reality, the sacred leadership became an esoteric, ingrown circle sustained by nepotism, favoritism, and patronage. The masquerade was accomplished in the best interest of the constituency, as though professionalism was genetic, not by merit and accomplishment or the uniqueness of the individual.

During the 1990's, members of the premajoritarian legal elite were no longer rail splitters nor minority business men, farmers, or even educated members of society. They were those who were born into households of economic and social privilege. With the right last name, wealth and resources of America, the world was their oyster, as only for them will neighborhood, education, and success be guaranteed. The local courthouse, law enforcement, and government officials shall function for them at the expense of any non-member of that elite class. The "dice are always loaded" in their favor by nepotism, favoritism, and patronage. Religion shall give its blessing on these practices because the ecclesiastical elite are like-minded and exempt themselves from a larger family. ("The King can do no wrong.")

In the 1770's, our forefathers understood this, and though not perfect, they determined in their genius that a representative republic based on the U.S. Constitution must commence. It did, and became the model for modern politics in the pursuit of fairness both in the sacred and secular. It was not perfect but there was the continual search for civilized fairness. However, the 1990's reveals that our representative republic is at the crossroads of sacred and secular notions of elitism, especially in the secular domain. The concept of sovereign immunity, ("The King can do no wrong,") poses a threat to our government.

Our forefathers understood this concept. That's why they came to America. Before their journey to North America, their habitats were dominated by classes of economic and social privilege. The economy and law did not function for the underprivileged because many of our forefathers struggled in circumstances where there was no heat, no shelter from the elements, no public education or basic medical care. Some even suffered starvation. Over time state religions gave their blessing to the intentional tyranny of the "Milords" and took on a new look---government became the oppressor. The king's rule sang the same tune with same old words, ("The King can do no wrong.")

In the 1990's we, who are the descendants of our forefathers, are confronted with the same crisis: we are involved in a government and circumstance, in both the sacred and the secular, where our institutions function only for the benefit of a social and economic privileged class. This process is an intentional exclusion of non-members. The alarm has sounded.

There are examples of this alarm in the sacred, such as ("Hail-Bop" and the Branch Davidians) as well as in the secular, (The Uni-Bomber and The Oklahoma Federal Building Bombing).

Our society needs a return to the republic, in both the sacred and the secular---a return in which the worth of a person is not measured by the possession of currency or reduced to a mercenary commodity for generating revenues and the making of money. Rather, the rights of a citizen must take precedence in the sacred and in the secular according to the U.S Constitution---the old one! Without a strong, thriving prosperous middle-class, the republic shall not survive into the next millennium, and the elitists in the sacred and the secular are being put on continual notice before it is too late.

1997

THE NATURAL WAY

By Gray Wolf

"You read the face of the sky and of the earth, but you have not recognized the one who is before you, and you do not know how to read this moment."

The Gospel of Thomas

For the sake of argument, let us say that life on Earth Mother is in a turmoil, with wars, deaths, fights, break-up of families, the destruction of home life, and the decay of moral life, in general. These are just some of the dire consequences evolving from man's egocentric actions to define who or what he is. Many different concepts have been made. Some insist that their way is the only way, and great conflict has resulted when others have disagreed or resisted.

Each country has its care-takers and each care-taker claims he has been told by the creator how to care for the country. These ways or rules of taking care of the country are carried on by the people to follow. I call these rules the "natural way."

The Native American accepts rules which are all rooted in the mysteries of life; they do not try to destroy, change, or run from them. Only when the Native American steps outside of his culture will his values change. Even then, he feels alone and left out, because he has strayed from his path.

Family values for a Native American are clannish. Relationship gives security and identity. The woman's place is the home as she is in closeness to Earth Mother. She is the cord that holds the family together. The male is supporter and provider for the family. He is protector and spiritual leader for his family. The children are supportive of the parents, not because of fear of punishment, but because of love and respect for the parents. These roles are never changed unless non-native values come into play.

Family values for non-Native Americans are based on who makes the most money and holds the greatest prestige. Where the woman makes the money, she rules the complete household while the man takes on the job of home-maker and child raising. The woman doesn't respect the man. The man resents the woman. The children, if they obey their parents at all, obey the parents out of fear of punishment.

Education for Native Americans is seen as a hands-on process or told by word of mouth and experienced in day-to-day life. Life morals are told in story form with a native twist. Education for non-native people is taught in schools by people who were taught in school, who most likely have never experienced anything of what they are teaching.

Peace for a Native American is to be in harmony with the entire cosmos. He honors the web of life and, if one thing is out of balance, he becomes out of balance.

For non-Native Americans personal harmony is sought inside the individual person. He doesn't care about anyone or anything as long as he is at peace. His greed overpowers his concern for anything. Ownership and property are communal to Native Americans, using only what is necessary at the time and owning only what is attached to the body. Even then, oftentimes, this is given or shared with others. Ownership to non-natives is legal ownership passed by law. Property is accumulated and stored to the point of surplus, the goods belonging to one person.

A sense of security and well-being for Native Americans is in what that person is about. This includes the wisdom they have gained, the years they have lived, and the children they have produced. He has reverence for nature. Security for non-native people is how much worldly goods they have saved, and the success they have achieved---"what have I done."

The Native American lives in the now. He cares not for tomorrow but strives to live a good life on a day-to-day basis, working when necessary and praying every waking day.

Non-native people live for tomorrow, looking forward to the American dream. They are always reaching out and putting off enjoyments for hopes of a better life, praying that one day they will get a rich reward that has been promised to them. In doing so, they lose the rewards of life that the Great Spirit gives them.

In closing, I would like to quote from a great native chief, Chief Seattle:

"When the last red man shall have perished, and the memory of my tribe shall have become a myth among the white man, these shores will swarm with the invisible dead of my tribe. .... At night when the streets of your cities are silent, and you think them deserted, they will throng with the returning host that once filled and loved this land. The white man will never be alone. Let him deal kindly with my people for the dead are not powerless. Dead, did I say? There are no deaths only a changing of worlds."

SUMMARY AS INSCAPE

"Keep walking, though there's no place to get to. Don't try to see through the distances. That's not for human beings. Move within, but don't move the way fear makes you move."

Rumi

Turney Center Industrial Prison and Farm is located near the town of Centerville, Tennessee. Captain Bubba Chandler told me that the late Grand Ole Opry comedian, Minnie Pearl, grew up there. The Captain also told me that she created the fictional hometown of Grinder's Switch. One family approached him on the street and asked, "Where do we find Grinder's Switch?" He directed them to a field right outside the town, and told them that they might find what's left of an old railroad track. He added, "It may not be what you're looking for." I can imagine this family going to this mythical place and looking into a landscape in which there is no physical Grinder's Switch. Suddenly, the landscape becomes what the 19th century English Jesuit poet Gerard Manley Hopkins calls an 'inscape'.

The correlative for subjective experience is inscape. Landscape, on the other hand, points to objective experience. Inscape carries what Hopkins calls impress---the force or impact associated with feeling and imagination. A person is moved by the power of words and ideas. Words and ideas have the power of carrying the tourist hundreds of miles to a place (Grinder's Switch) not situated in physical space or in time. Some enter that inscape and come out feeling betrayed

147

or disappointed; others come out feeling refreshed, pleasantly surprised, invigorated, in wonder.

We are always in story, moving from the past, into the present and on into the future. We understand when Minnie Pearl creates a fiction from her personal past history and shares it with the world.

We are always in one physical landscape or another. This is not the case with our fictions; story takes us into those imaginative possibilities referred to as inscape. Objectively speaking, it is 'not-yet.' If the impress is strong enough, we may find ourselves living out the story.

It is easy to believe that these stories move a person or persons into action. That's what advertising or propaganda is about. They are efforts to move our behavior.

What about stumbling into a very powerful life-changing experience---one that contains impress. The family that traveled to Centerville, Tennessee (Grinder's Switch) were obviously moved by the story.

Victor Hugo's classic book *Les Misérables*, tells of a man just released from prison who makes the choice to live out his life-changing experience. The book has been turned into a movie and is now out on Blue Ray and DVD.

At the beginning of the movie, Jean Valjean, the hero, is released from nineteen years of hard labor in prison. He is making his way to check in with his parole officer and is directed by a peasant to find food, shelter and rest with a bishop and his wife who live in a community along the way. The bishop takes the ragged and rough-looking Jean Valjean into his home. Before the night has ended, the bishop catches Valjean in the act of stealing a set of silverware. In the process of this robbery, the bishop is struck down by the thief.

The following morning, two officers apprehended a vagabond, Jean Valjean, with a cache of silver. Valjean's story to the officers is that the silverware had been a gift from the bishop. The officers and Valjean enter the bishop's garden to check out the story. Valjean is utterly surprised when the bishop lies by immediately agreeing that the

148

silverware had been a gift. In addition, the bishop gives Jean Valjean two silver candlesticks worth 2000 francs. Jean Valjean is set free of his chains and the officers of the law leave the scene. In fear and trembling, the bishop removes the hood from the thief's head and looks him squarely in the eye.

"Don't forget," says the bishop, "don't ever forget that you've promised to become a new man."

In fear and trembling, Jean Valjean asks, "Why are you doing this?"

The bishop replies, "Jean Valjean, my brother, you no longer belong to me. With this silver I've bought your soul. I've ransomed you from fear and hatred, and now I give you back to God."

Nineteen years of hard labor in prison has not taught him forgiveness or pardon. Suddenly and unexpectedly, he is now faced with a new possibility, pardon. Jean Valjean is faced with his own subjectivity---the choice to live as a 'new man.' The bishop has ransomed him from fear and hatred. He has given Valjean back to God. The choice rests solidly on the shoulders of Jean Valjean. The impress of the experience is profound. It carries Valjean into a new life free of crime and hatred. It is a convictional moment.

A story, a signpost, a measuring rod in the objective world may not be enough to bring one to a transforming moment where conviction is sufficient to make a deep and lasting change in a person's character. The bishop has no external guarantee that the thief will change. His choice to suspend the ethical by lying is a leap of faith. Neither does Valjean have an external guarantee that his new life will have its rewards. His choice is an act of faith. Jean Valjean has been pardoned and, in the course of the movie, he gives pardon.

The story, Les Misérables, is about a character who lives into his narrative and undergoes transformation. The element of subjectivity makes good Christian storytelling problematic; there is difficulty in judging the direction of another person's motives and intentions. The outcome is not certain or guaranteed. For example, a story included in this book entitled, "A Surprise Reunion," is about a young man named Ben who receives a book from a stranger. Interestingly, Ben's intentions and motives are in line with his personal history. The outcome is unexpected and surprising. Who would think that the gift of a book would have such unexpected consequences? In a surprise reunion, he meets a prisoner, the man who gave him the book that changed his life. Ben is naturally brought into a life-changing event that reflects what took place ten years earlier. Ben came to prison as a volunteer, not with any intention to serve himself. A Buddhist would say he came with no gaining idea. Rather, he came looking for men to teach, hoping to empower them for transformation. "For whosoever will save his life shall lose it: but whosoever will lose his life for my sake, the same shall save it" (Lu 9:24). Ben's encounter is fleshed out in history and, at the same time, very symbolic---mystical.

This lived experience is like a story within a story. Ben's story is imbedded in the *Parable of the Ten Virgins*. To witness this event in the light of the parable presents itself as a life choice.

It is like being somewhere between the objectivity of a landscape and the subjectivity of an inscape. On the one hand, what happened has a factual, objective history. On the other hand, you are moved, shocked, taken back, by the incredible coincidence of events. The question that comes to mind is: "What does one do with such an event? Do you call in a coincidence squad to identify it as such and then move on?" What one does with that event is a subjective move. For me, it was a convictional moment---one that I associated with the *Parable of the Ten Virgins*. I made the connection and, therefore, brought the Christian gospel to my experience. My faith is strengthened through these gifts of the Spirit—these transforming moments. These surprise experiences call my attention to a living Kingdom, an inscape, beyond mere objective comprehension. The impress of it is powerful and moving, driving me or anyone else into the choice of renewed living.

Imagination is hard to kill. In the prison environment imagination is like bellows set before smoldering embers. In the story, "The Calling," I am simply walking to unit 5 and, without being conscious of it, I go from landscape to inscape. Suddenly, I realize that something is off. Looking back, I can say that it was surreal. There is a Christlike figure sitting cross-legged on concrete surrounded by what looks like devotees who are also sitting cross-legged on concrete. Suddenly, I discover that this young stranger knows me and tells me that he knows none of the men who surround him. The bellows are on the fire. They begin to pump; the embers begin to glow. Imagination is at work.

A perfect example of moving unawares into an imaginative inscape is in the story, "Captain to the Bridge." A psychotic inmate, trapped in his imagination, is living in a cell filled with his own feces. The chaplain peers through the pie-flap. The stench, the squalor, tells him that something is way out of the ordinary. The inmate's imagination has carried him to a very dark place. The inmate calls out, "Captain to the bridge." The chaplain replies, "Bridge to the captain." Their imaginations connect; their stories link. The inmate undergoes decontamination. No one hearing the story can forget it. The image has impress. The bellows are on the fire.

Living into an inscape is like entering a labyrinth. Entering into the executions of Sedley Alley and Cecil Johnson is to experience a place where, at first, you think that there is no way out. Moving through the maze, we discovered threads, objective threads or crumbs, that suggest a way out: Sedley Alley's dream, a skunk, a pigeon, a football game, a phone call, a rejection, a winning touchdown and, finally, the faith of an inmate. Faith in God opens up the doors of possibility. Through God all things are possible (Mt 19:26).

People recognize this thread and are afraid. They keep at a safe distance. An administrative captain---most likely the executioner, who smells the skunk in prison air after the execution of Sedley Alley---catches the thread, but lets it go. There is the woman who participates in an execution and loses her baby, or the man who goes into the death chamber alone to work on the sound system and falls through the ceiling. This employee hangs upside down long enough to lose his sight. "Urban legends are not real threads," so it is said. Such legends are turns of a collective imagination gone amok.

At this point, I have to ask myself the question: "What is the most important thread that I've gathered from my prison experience?" There are many threads in this tapestry, making a *Fellowship of the Thread* woven together with inmates, staff and volunteers. This fellowship is a shared story which brings new life to all of us.

During our study group at Turney Center, I brought in Carol Pearson's book on archetypes. What we learned to do from her book was to recognize an image of organization such as a Warrior, a Caregiver or a Lover. We even made up images up like the Romantic. The men seemed to delight in seeing into each other through these images. In the story, "Learning is Reciprocal," Phillip is the Romantic. Joe, who saw himself as a hermetic character, also claimed to be a polytheist. What was so amazing is that no one got offended by the various insights of the group. Even, Major Phelps, after being characterized as a 'closet fundamentalist,' laughed it off. They all shared their stories. I am delighted to have shared some of these stories and writings with you.

On my wall hangs a not-so-politically-correct award given to me by those in prison. Beside my mug-shot, it reads: HONORARY CONVICT. This award was given to me on the month of my retirement, August 2011. It states that I am "now a fully vested and certifiable convict." The award concludes: "From this day forward, you are the marginalized, oppressed, and outcast of society."

In the story, "Can People Choose How They Cross Over," Harold Weatherford wanted to go out preaching and did. I never really thought about how I wanted to go out until now. My mother would have been pleased with HONORARY RESIDENT, but HONORARY CONVICT! I don't think so. The gift of HONORARY CONVICT is a perfect way to end. It is an inscape that my mother would never have imagined.

Epilogue

At the time of this writing, Don Johnson is scheduled to be executed by the state of Tennessee at 7 PM on May 16, 2019. I had previously written the governor asking him to grant Don clemency. Don had been convicted for the murder of his wife, Connie, in 1984. In early March of 2019, Rev. Charles Fels visited our home in College Grove, Tennessee. Rev. Fels was well aware of Don's conversion and his reconciliation with his step-daughter, Cynthia Vaughn. He asked If I would support an effort to save Don's life. I wrote the following letter to friends and volunteers who had served at the Riverbend Maximum Security Prison in Nashville. The following letter went out:

Dear Friends,

This note is to those who have served in prison ministry and believe that life is sacred. Don Johnson, who some of you may know, is scheduled to be executed at 7:00 p.m. on May 16, 2019.

I met Don in 1989 when the Riverbend Maximum Security Institution opened its doors. Don spent over thirty years on death row. He has built and nourished many relationships over the years. Don is an ordained Christian minister in the Seventh Day Adventist church.

Don's loss of life would be a loss for all of us. Therefore, I am asking you to write Governor Bill Lee and ask him to grant Don clemency.

While serving as chaplain at Riverbend, I came to know that the Governor supported prison ministry. One of our former residents, Wayne Bratcher, worked at Bill Lee's company after being released from prison. Wayne started a ministry and later became a volunteer on death row. It is hopeful that the Governor will see his way to release Don from the death penalty. However, he needs to hear this from you.

Please see the enclosed attachment. This attachment tells how to speak out and has the governor's address. Please send a copy of anything you send to the Governor to Don's clemency counsel, Rev. Charles Fels' address is also listed on the attachment.

When I returned as an interim chaplain in 2014, Don told me that his step-daughter had visited him and they were finally at peace with one another. Two of our volunteers, Richard Gardner and Wayne Bratcher, prayed with Don over the letters sent to Cynthia. Their prayers were heard. You can witness these and other testimonies at the website www.faithforgivenessredemption.com.

There is another issue that has recently come to the forefront concerning the conviction and execution of Sedley Alley. Did the state execute an innocent man? Here is a quote from Tennesseans for Alternatives to the Death Penalty (TAPD):

Today, April Alley, the daughter of Sedley Alley, announced that she is petitioning the Shelby County Criminal Court in Memphis for the post-conviction DNA testing of the evidence in her father's case. Ms. Alley is also asking Governor Bill Lee to use his executive authority to order DNA testing of the untested evidence.

Tennessee executed Sedley Alley in 2006 after he was convicted for the 1985 rape and murder of Marine Lance Corporal Suzanne Marie Collins. DNA evidence from the crime scene was not tested in 1985 and has never been tested. Berry Scheck, co-founder of the Innocence Project, and Vanessa Potkin, post-conviction litigation director for the Innocence Project, represent Ms. Alley.

Again, Governor Bill Lee is being asked to exercise his executive authority. The question of guilt or innocence does not depend on faith; it depends on accepting or rejecting the evidence. The question of redemption and transformation is a construct that rests on faith. Christian faith is a choice that one must buy into and take on. Faith takes courage because it challenges the discourse of a broken world.

In 1965, Governor Frank Clement exercised his executive authority and commuted the execution of five men. Three of these men were sentenced to die in the electric chair on the following day. Governor Clement prayed over his decision and took on the courage to proclaim his faith.

May 2, 2019

Postscript

Having executive privilege, the governor literally holds the power of life and death, with two choices: To be a visionary and take the road less travelled or to go with the crowd and the way of death.

Doing the right thing is never easy. There is a force for maintaining the status quo versus having the wisdom and courage to make a choice for change and transformation. This decision for the governor is a convictional challenge.

In the introduction to this book, I am confronted by an inmate who asks, "Chaplain, who do you work for?" I told him that I was employed by the State of Tennessee. The inmate corrected me, "No, Chaplain, you work for God!" I would ask the governor the same question, "Who do you work for?" I've lived into that question and now I know who I am writing for--God!

Chaplain Jerry Welborn
May 5, 2019